MORE TALKS FOR CHILDREN

More
Talks for Children

EDITED BY
Ian MacLeod

WITH CONTRIBUTIONS FROM

Richard Coley
David Harbison
Iain MacDonald
Ian Roy
Beatrice Surtees

Saint Andrew Press
EDINBURGH

First published in 1992 by
SAINT ANDREW PRESS
121 George Street, Edinburgh EH2 4YN

ISBN 0 7152 0657 5

British Library Cataloguing-in-Publication Data
 More talks for children.
  I. MacLeod, Ian
  248

  ISBN: 0715206575

Printed and bound by Athenaeum Press Ltd, Newcastle upon Tyne.

Contents

PART 2: SCHOOL WORSHIP *by Iain MacDonald*

FOREWORD

More Talks for Children is a sequel to *Talks for Children* and I am grateful to the publishing manager and committee of Saint Andrew Press for the invitation to edit and contribute to this new volume. Thanks are also due to the five other contributors: Mrs Beatrice Surtees, who was co-author with me on the first book; the Revd Richard Coley of Tollcross Victoria Church, Glasgow; the Revd David Harbison of Beith High Church; and the Revd Ian Roy of Livingstone Church, Stevenston. A special word of thanks must be said to the Revd Iain MacDonald, who, until retirement last year, was Adviser in Religious Education to the Glasgow Area of Strathclyde Region. I am grateful to him for sharing his expertise on the subject of the School Assembly, and for practical examples of how it might best be conducted. Many ministers, vaguely aware of both educational theory and of changes in society which are reflected in our schools, know that the School Assembly should be 'different', but are uncertain as to how to go about it. Iain MacDonald's article in Part 2 of this book therefore should prove of particular value.

Gratitude should also be expressed to the Editor of the *Expository Times* for permission to reprint several stories which first appeared there. They are: 'The Light' by Richard Coley (October issue 1987: *page* 15), 'The Cold Shoulder' by Ian MacLeod (June 1989: *page* 340), 'The Extraordinary in the Ordinary' by Ian MacLeod (November 1988: *page* 56).

The sincere hope of all the contributors is that these talks may be of use to colleagues in the ministry and to those who require to conduct worship in school.

Ian MacLeod 1991

ACKNOWLEDGMENT

The Editor gratefully acknowledges Arthur Mee's
The Children's Encyclopaedia
from which
'THE STRUGGLE AND THE BLESSING' (p 22) is adapted.

PART 1

MORE TALKS FOR CHILDREN

THE
JOHN O' GROATS SIGNPOST

TEXT: PSALM 90:1

Lord, thou hast been our dwelling place in all generations.

I wonder if you have ever visited John O' Groats in the far north of Scotland? If you have, then you will know that, standing on the headland, there is a fascinating signpost which has many arms.

One arm tells you that you are 3500 miles from New York. Another that you are 1500 miles from Moscow. Another tells that if you want to go to the North Pole you would have 7200 miles to go. And yet others that Land's End is 876 miles off, and the distance to London is 690 miles.

One specially interesting thing about John O' Groats is that, beside the signpost, there is usually a photographer at work, anxious to take pictures of the tourists.

Whenever a customer approaches him, he will ask, 'Where do you come from?' Then, on being told, he will look up a little book and make a calculation. Finally, before taking the photograph of the happy visitor, he will delve into a little box with letters and numbers in it, slide them into a new arm which he has made for the signpost, and attach the arm very carefully to the post so that it looks as though it belongs there among all the others. That done, a visitor, or a whole crowd of visitors, can have a photograph taken from the John O' Groats signpost, which now clearly shows the name of their own home town, and how many miles away from it they are when standing on the headland in John O' Groats.

When I saw the photographer in action, I couldn't help saying to myself, 'I wonder how far it is from John O' Groats to my home?' That's when I found myself asking a deeper question: 'Where is my *real* home?'

The Psalmist had a lovely thought when he said, 'Lord, You have been our dwelling place in all generations.' He was saying that God is our home.

One of our poets, William Wordsworth, said the same thing:

But trailing clouds of glory do we come
From God who is our home.

Now if God is our true home, boys and girls, what a pity that we do not have a signpost to point the way home! That is why I am very glad that I belong to an organisation called the Church. For in every village and town and city there is a church, just like the one in which we worship this morning. Wherever it is, and, whether it is a little village church, a large town church, or a great cathedral with a towering spire, the church is the signpost that points the way for us all. The only difference is that far from telling us how far away we are from home, it tells us how near God is to us all.

PRAYER

Father, we thank you for the church with its message of your love which is made known to us in Jesus. Help us, day by day, to live in the knowledge that we belong to you, that you are our true home, and that we are loved and cared for by you. In Jesus' name.

Amen

DEAD SLOW HORSES

TEXT: MATTHEW 11:15

He who has ears to hear, let him hear.

There is a certain hotel in Scotland to which, for several reasons, ministers often go for a holiday. It is a very large hotel in the town of Crieff, surrounded by the lovely Perthshire countryside. Set in spacious grounds, it has a swimming pool, tennis and squash courts, a golf course, bowling green, riding stables, croquet lawn, and lots of other attractions besides. There ministers often meet colleagues whom they have not met before, and others whom they have not seen for a long period of time, so that friendships are made and renewed as many a story is exchanged.

Some time ago, while I was on holiday at that hotel, I was driving from the golf course past a field where the horses from the riding stables are left to graze. Just for a moment, I couldn't believe my eyes. For there, at the side of the road, was a notice which read, 'DEAD SLOW HORSES!'

Now that seemed to me a strange notice to place near a riding stable. I mean, I am no horseman. But if I were, I doubt if I would want to hire a 'dead slow horse.' Were I a rider, I should want a horse of which I could be proud—a noble steed with his head high in the air, and certainly one with the ability to trot and canter and occasionally break out into a gallop at my command. I should want an animal with a stately stride, one that is swift and fleet of foot. The idea of 'DEAD SLOW HORSES' made no appeal to me, and I said so to my wife.

4

But of course, as my wife wisely pointed out, the words on the sign 'DEAD SLOW HORSES' were not there to advertise the horses in the stables. Nor were they even intended for those who wanted to go riding. I was too dull to see it, but they were there for me, and for any other people like me who happened to drive down the road. The notice had been placed as a warning to motorists to exercise care. It was a reminder that horses and their riders could very well cross the path, so drivers must give them the consideration due. 'DEAD SLOW HORSES' applied to me.

How easy it is, boys and girls, to imagine that sound words, good advice and even warnings which are given, somehow apply to other people but not to ourselves. That is why Jesus often said, after he had finished telling a story, 'He who has ears to hear, let him hear.' It was another way of saying, 'This means you.'

When we come to worship on Sunday mornings, let's remember that the words of the hymns, the prayers, the Bible reading and the sermon, are not meant for everyone else while they have nothing to say to us. Before every part of the service we need to remember the words of Jesus: 'He who has ears to hear, let him hear'—This means you!

PRAYER

Lord, as we worship, help us to remember that you are ready to speak to us. Give us ears which are attentive, that we may be as ready to hear, and, having heard, be ready to obey. In Jesus' name.

Amen

NEEDLE IN A HAYSTACK

TEXT: PSALM 139:2

Thou knowest when I sit down and when I rise up.

How would you like to look for 'a needle in a haystack'? That is a phrase we sometimes use when a desk, say, or a room, is all in a clutter and we are looking for something which we know is nearby, but are unable to find it. 'It's like looking for a needle in a haystack,' we say.

This is a very descriptive phrase, and I had always thought, until recent times, that the 'needle' was a sewing or darning needle. Now I know differently, for I was watching the 'Jim'll Fix It' programme on television some time ago, when two young girls wrote to Jimmy Saville asking him to 'fix' it for them to look for a 'needle in a haystack.'

Taken to a farm, they first helped the farmer to build a gigantic haystack. Like the old fashioned haystacks, it was very long and very high—almost as long and high as our church—so that they could only reach the top by a ladder. Then the farmer showed them a 'needle.' But the needle was not a sewing or darning needle. It was a metal rod about two metres long, with a ring-shaped handle to give a firm grip, and the farmer explained that the 'needle' is a tool used for pulling a sample of hay from the stack.

Then, while the girls covered their eyes, he buried the 'needle' in the haystack and their search began. But after poking all round the hay for a long time, they could not find it. In the end, they only managed to locate it with the help of a metal detector!

6

Looking for 'a needle in a haystack' is still a painstaking task, even when the 'needle' is two metres long!

Sometimes when we think of the vastness of the universe and the millions who live on our planet earth, we think that for God to know anything about us at all must be like looking for 'a needle in a haystack.' There is a Psalm in the Bible in which the writer tells us that we can never be hidden from God. Indeed the Psalmist even says to God, 'You know when I sit down and when I rise up.' It is a very wonderful thought that God's knowledge of us and his care for us is as great as that, so that we can never be just 'a needle in a haystack' to him.

PRAYER

Father, we praise you, that you care for each of us as individuals, so that with you we are never just one of a crowd. Help us to respond to your love with lives which are pleasing to you. In Jesus' name.
Amen

LIGHTING-UP TIME

VISUAL AIDS

A candle, and a small jam jar which is large enough to cover the candle.

TEXT: MATTHEW 5:15-16

Nor do men light a lamp and put it under a bushel, but on a stand and it gives light to all in the house. Let your light so shine before men, that they may see your good works and give glory to your Father who is in heaven.

Today, boys and girls, we are going to try an experiment, and then I shall tell you a story.

These words of Jesus were about a light and a bushel. We all know what a light is, and we are going to provide a light with this candle. (*Light candle which is placed on a flat surface.*) Maybe, on the other hand, you don't know what a bushel is. A bushel was a container used in the days of Jesus, probably made of earthenware. It was used for measuring the grain needed for baking bread. Every house in Palestine would have a bushel. Now I don't have a bushel this morning, but I do have something like a bushel, though it is very much smaller. In fact, for our purposes it's even better than a bushel, for, being made of glass, we can see through it. (*Hold up jam jar.*)

What was it that Jesus said? 'No man lights a lamp and puts it under a bushel.' Let's see what happens when I put my light under the bushel. (*Place jam jar over candle, which will extinguish within a few seconds.*) There you are, boys and girls. That is what happens when we put a light under a bushel. It goes out. That is why Jesus said, 'No man lights a lamp and puts it under a bushel.' If anybody did that, the lamp would eventually go out, just as ours did, even though, because the bushel was larger, it would have taken much longer. Jesus said that the proper thing to do with a lamp was to put it 'on a stand, and it gives light to all in the house.'

Now for the story.

Many, many years ago in the city of London, there was no public lighting, so that when the sun had set, the city was in darkness. The City Fathers, however, aware of the dangers of unlit streets, devised a plan so that householders themselves would provide light for every passer-by. The plan was that each house of £10 rental, which faced outwards onto a street or a lane, should display a lantern on a hook fixed to the house wall. This had to be done from from six o'clock until eleven o'clock at night, during the dark months of September to March. Every night the watchman ensured that it was done by going round the streets in the early evening, crying, 'Hang out your lights.' For many years that is how London was lit at night. It was lit by each householder playing a part in the lighting of the city.

Jesus expected his followers to do something like that. He who was himself the light of the world, told his disciples that they too were the light of the world. That is to say, that they were to reflect the light of the love and faith and goodness that they had seen in him. As long as each disciple played his part and 'hung out his light', then the world would be full of the light that was found in Jesus. If any disciple failed to 'hang out his lamp,' or 'hid his light under a bushel,' then that corner of the world would be dark.

The people of London only 'hung out their lamps' at night time and during the winter months. Jesus asks his followers to reflect his love and faith and goodness *everyday* and *all of* the time. 'Let your light so shine before men,' he says, 'that they may see your good works and give glory to your Father who is in heaven.' Boys and girls, it is lighting-up time. Will *you* hang out your lamps?

THINGS TO DO

1 Find out the kind of lamps which were used in Palestine in Jesus' day.
2 Ask your teacher if, together, you might make one.

PRAYER

Father, we thank you for the light of love and faith and goodness which we have seen in Jesus. Help us day by day to reflect that light, so that others may find the way to you. In Jesus' name.
Amen

The Cold Shoulder

TEXT: JOHN 6:37

. . . him who comes to me I will not cast out.

I wonder if you have ever been given the 'cold shoulder'? Or, even worse, I wonder if you have ever given the 'cold shoulder' to somebody else? Have you ever heard anybody use that expression? Does anybody know what it means? Well, to give somebody the 'cold shoulder' means to act towards them in an unfriendly manner, to treat them indifferently as if they do not matter, to make it perfectly plain that you have little time for them.

But where did such a strange expression come from and how did it find its way into our common speech? The answer, it seems, goes back to the days of chivalry, that is, to the days of knights in shining armour, to what we call the 'Middle Ages.' In those days it was expected that a knight would always give a welcome to any fellow knight who came to visit him. Indeed, not only was he expected to give him a welcome, but to give him board and lodgings too, with the finest food and drink that he could provide. And further, he was expected to do that for as long as the visiting knight chose to stay.

Sometimes, of course, a knight played on this hospitality and took advantage of the custom by overstaying his welcome, until the knight who was doing the entertaining longed for his fellow knight to go away. So, when that happened, the host would instruct his kitchen no longer to serve the very best of food and drink, but to offer in its place cold shoulder of mutton which was regarded, at the time, as meat only fit for servants. And when a visiting knight, therefore, was served with cold shoulder, he knew that the time had come for him to leave. So perhaps you can see why the phrase is still used when one person shows himself unfriendly to another. That is to give him the 'cold shoulder.'

One person who never gave the 'cold shoulder' was Jesus. The Gospels tell us how people came to him day and night—people who were sick or anxious or who simply wanted their questions answered—and Jesus always had time for them. Better still, Jesus welcomes and always has time for people like you and me. In his own words he said, 'him who comes to me I will not cast out.'

THINGS TO DO

1   Think of any other expressions we commonly use, and try to find out where they came from.
2   Think of any particular groups of people who may possibly be without friends, and how me might befriend them.
3   Read the story of a man who was being given the 'cold shoulder', but whom Jesus befriended (See Luke 19:1-9).

PRAYER

Lord Jesus Christ, we thank you that you have time for every one of us. Help us, like you, to be ready to befriend those who are lonely and to try to bring them joy.

Amen

THE LANGUAGE OF LOVE

TEXT: JOHN 13:35

By this all men will know that you are my disciples, if you have love for one another.

Have you ever thought how strange it is that there are so many different languages in the world? The fact that there are makes understanding people from other countries and races so difficult. We call it a language barrier.

Perhaps you have discovered this problem if you have gone 'abroad' for a holiday. It is always exciting, of course, to visit places like France or Germany or Italy or Spain, or countries even farther away. There is so much to see and learn. But how much easier that would be if only we could speak the languages of the countries we visit. Few things are more frustrating than to hear people speak, but to be unable to understand what they are saying; and to speak to people who cannot understand what we say, because there is a language barrier between us.

Many people have thought about that barrier and how it might be broken down. One way, which most of us have tried in other countries, is to use a kind of sign language, so that in a shop, for example, we will point with our finger to what we want, or perform a little mime, hoping that the shopkeeper will understand. Usually it works, although sometimes it has the most comical results! But it is impossible by that means to have any kind of conversation. A much better way, of course, is to learn other languages besides our own. Some of you will do that at school

13

and that is very worthwhile. But there are so many different languages in the world that even the most clever person could only learn a few. That is why some have thought how wonderful it would be were there one universal language which all of us could speak and understand.

Several attempts to create such a language have been made and probably the most well known is a language which is called 'Esperanto.' Esperanto was the work of a Russian scholar called Dr Zamenhof, and he published his language just over one hundred years ago in 1887. It is made up of words and sounds common to all the European countries, but deliberately leaves out whatever is special to any one of them. Dr Zamenhof, having created his new language, wrote a poem in it and about it. Translated into English, it said that by sharing a common language and 'understanding one another, the peoples shall form, in agreement, one great family circle.'

That was a great aim, boys and girls. Little wonder that he called his new language 'Esperanto', for the word comes from the Spanish word for 'hope', and Esperanto was written as a language with the great hope behind it that the peoples of the world would be united in a family because they could speak a common tongue.

Another who believed in a universal language was Jesus and he wanted all his followers to use it. That is why he said, 'By this all men will know that you are my disciples, if you have love for one another.' Jesus knew well that, even if we all spoke the same language, words can still be misunderstood. He wanted us to speak the language of love, for caring actions and loving deeds can be understood wherever we are and wherever we go. They mark us out as disciples of Jesus. Do you and I speak the universal language which he taught us?

THINGS TO DO

1 Make a list of the different languages of the world that you
   know of.
2 Consult a map to see the countries where these are spoken.

PRAYER

*Father, we remember that it was said of Jesus, your Son, that 'he
went about doing good.' Help us so to follow his good example that
we may be worthy to be called his disciples.*

Amen

THE EXTRAORDINARY IN THE ORDINARY

VISUAL AIDS

One ordinary Christmas card, one humourous Christmas card and one musical Christmas card.

TEXT: COLOSSIANS 1:15

He is the image of the invisible God.

For most boys and girls this is an exciting time of the year, and, whenever the postman calls, more and more Christmas cards arrive in our homes. I sometimes wonder what makes a person send a particular kind of card.

Here is a very plain card, although in spite of its plainness it is still attractive. It has no picture at all and it simply says 'Christmas Greetings.' Perhaps the people who sent it were a little tired of horse-drawn coaches and village churches deep in snow and people ice skating on the pond. They simply wanted to send their good wishes and the plain card serves the purpose well.

Here is another one. (*Display the humourous card explaining why it appeals to you.*) This kind of card was probably chosen by someone who enjoys laughter and wants to make others laugh too. It certainly made me laugh when I opened it and read it!

Here is another card, boys and girls. Just looking at it, it doesn't seem very special, does it? But let's open it. (*Let music play.*) Now isn't that wonderful? What seemed at first sight a very ordinary card, is really quite extraordinary because it contains the

16

most wonderful music. I imagine the sender chose this card because he or she wanted their greeting to be 'special.'

I think people are a bit like that Christmas card. Sometimes those we meet can seem so ordinary, but then, as their lives open out to us, we discover that they have abilities and talents and personalities which are very wonderful and which enrich our lives!

That was true, most of all, of Jesus. How ordinary a baby born in a cattle shed must have seemed to people! How ordinary a carpenter working in a village shop! But as his life opened out to them and they saw the things that he said and did, some realised that his was the most wonderful life of all, showing the very heart and mind and character of God. That is why one of them wrote the words, 'He is the image of the invisible God.'

PRAYER

Father, we praise you that Jesus came to live the kind of life that we have to live. Even more we praise you that he has shown us how it should be lived. Help us to see his life as the pattern and example which we should follow.

Amen

DIARIES

I wonder if, at the beginning of a year, you have ever been presented with a brand new diary and then resolved to make an entry in it every single day? We all know what happens. We manage to do it for the first few days then we have a late night and are too tired, so we make up the missing entry the next night. Then all goes well for the next few days, until we have another late night, when again we miss an entry. Then comes another and another, and before we know it, our good intention has gone!

But it is a great thing to keep a diary. Some have become famous for having done that very thing. One well known diary is that of Samuel Pepys who wrote about the London he knew in the time of King Charles II, and about his experiences as secretary to the Admiralty. Another is that of John Evelyn, who wrote, among other things, about the Great Fire of London. Yet another, which many boys and girls have read, is the diary of Ann Frank, who hid from the Nazis in Amsterdam during the Second World War.

Lots of ministers kept diaries too, and some of them are fascinating to read hundreds of years after they were written. One, published by the Scottish History Society about a hundred years ago, is the diary of a minister who lived in the Shetland Islands from 1712-1806. His name was John Mill and what an exciting story he had to tell!

John Mill lived through the Jacobite rebellion of 1745, when Bonnie Prince Charlie and his Highlanders tried to take over the throne of this country. John Mill was not, himself, a supporter of the Prince, but the landowner of his parish was, and John Mill tells how he was shut out of his own church for weeks until the rebellion was over and Bonnie Prince Charlie was on his way back to France.

The reason for this was that the landowner would allow no prayers for King George to be said in the church.

John Mill also lived through the American War of Independence and the French Revolution, although he had very few kind things to say about the revolutionaries in either country.

He also lived at the time when the pressgangs operated, forcing men into naval service, and he tells how some of the crofter-fishermen of his parish were captured by them.

Mill also lived at the time of the discovery of Australia, and he tells how Captain Cook saw an animal in that country, which is called in his diary, a 'Kangoura', but which we know better as the kangaroo.

But there is a more thrilling entry in John Mill's diary when one day, he wrote in it, 'I love Jesus Christ above all, and it is my heart's desire to follow him faithfully all my days.'

It is a wonderful thing to keep a diary, boys and girls. Better still if we can write in our diary what John Mill wrote in his: 'I love Jesus Christ above all, and it is my heart's desire to follow him faithfully all my days.' Best of all if, like that minister of long ago, we can be faithful for a whole lifetime, not just in keeping a diary but in being true to Jesus our Lord.

PRAYER

Father, as another year begins, help us to begin it determined that through all its days, happy or sad, we will faithfully follow Jesus. Our prayer we ask in his name.

Amen

THE ROGUE CLOCK

TEXT: JOHN 9:4

We must work the works of him who sent me, while it is day; night comes, when no one can work.

I wonder if you ever watch the news on television or hear it read on the radio? I always think that our newsreaders are people who deserve our admiration. One day, if you visit a broadcasting studio, you will understand what I mean.

All our news programmes, after all, are broadcast 'live', and are not recorded in advance. That means that newsreaders cannot afford to make mistakes, and mercifully they seldom do, for there is no way of correcting errors on a 'live' programme. It has always to be 'right first time.' It also means that the news items must be read at exactly the right speed—not too quickly, so that listeners will be unable to make out what is said, and not too slowly either—for the programme must finish on time, allowing the next one to begin just when it should.

Some time ago Mr Charles Carroll, one of the newsreaders at BBC Radio Bedfordshire, had a dreadful experience. He was reading the news on a 'live' broadcast, and, now and again like all newsreaders, he would glance at the clock in the studio which helped him to keep reading to time. That day, however, the electric clock above him had developed a serious fault and the hands were travelling around the dial at twice the normal speed. Because he was unaware of it, Mr Carroll had only two and a half minutes to read a programme which should have lasted for five. So he made

20

a heroic effort to speak twice as quickly as normal, until eventually he found himself quite out of breath and having to miss out some of the items which should have been read.

I hope the BBC rewarded poor Mr Carroll for a very brave effort. It wasn't his fault that the clock had turned rogue. Who would ever expect to find a faulty clock in a broadcasting studio?

For you and me, of course, time does not travel at twice its normal speed, although sometimes, when we are enjoying ourselves, it may well seem like that. For us, time is carefully measured by the clock. Nevertheless it is always precious and we have to learn to use it with care. Each of us only has a certain amount of time and it is wise, therefore, never to waste it or to spend it on useless things. Jesus was always aware of how valuable time is and he once said, 'We must work the works of him who sent me, while it is day; night comes, when no one can work.' For Jesus, the best way to spend time was in doing the things that God wanted done in the world—performing deeds of kindness, love and mercy. He expected his followers to do that too. What better way for any of us to use the time that we have.

THINGS TO DO

Within a group, and using the experiences of the children during a week, make up a short news broadcast, which one of the children should read within, say, two minutes.

PRAYER

Father, help us to use the time we have wisely. Above all, help us so to use it that we have time for others and for you. In Jesus' name.
Amen

THE STRUGGLE
AND THE BLESSING

There is an old story told by the Chippeway Indians, of the days when they knew nothing of growing food and they survived by hunting animals.

One day a fourteen year old boy of the tribe was led by his father into the woods. Soon they came to a spot where the father stopped, built a small wigwam for the boy and told him that he would return with food in a week. It was time for his son, by Chippeway custom, to make his preparation for life ahead by thinking and fasting on his own.

When his father had gone the boy felt very lonely. But he prayed to the Great Spirit and, in his prayer, he asked not for fame or fortune, but only that he might have the power to make life easier for others.

By the third day, since he had taken no food, the boy was weak, so that he could only lie in a daze. Suddenly the flap of his wigwam opened and a young Indian brave came in. His feathered head-dress, cloak and moccasins were green. His voice was like the sound of the wind through the trees. 'The Great Spirit has listened to your prayers,' he said. 'I have been sent to test your courage, and you must stand and wrestle with me.'

The boy rose and between the two there was a long struggle, not a word being spoken until at last the visitor said he would leave and return the next night. The following evening he returned and again they struggled, but now the young lad, whose prayer the Great Spirit had heard, seemed to gain strength from the very touch of his opponent. This time, the brave dressed in green praised him and promised to return. On the third night he came again and the same thing happened.

When the last night of his fast came, the young Indian lad was exhausted, but he squared up to his visitor the moment he arrived. As their arms joined in combat, his strength was renewed. In fact, as they wrestled, he grew so strong that he threw his opponent to the ground. Then as he stood back, staring down at his victim, the proud look on his face turned to horror when he saw that the brave in green was dying. Suddenly the dying warrior spoke, and as he spoke he smiled. 'Do not be sad,' he said. 'If you want me to live again, and see my green head-dress once more, you must bury me, and make sure that my grave is covered with clean, moist earth. When I have slept enough, I will break through the earth towards the sun.'

Sadly, the fasting young Indian obeyed. When his father returned to take him home, he said nothing of his sad story. He returned regularly, nevertheless, to attend his friend's grave.

One day, after a week of hunting, the Indian lad found the grave carpeted in green. Going closer, he saw it was covered with broad leaves of a kind he had never seen before, and he quietly wondered and did not disturb them. Then came a day when golden tassels fell from the leaves and the boy ran for his father. The older brave came, looked and thought deeply for a moment. Then he said, 'This is a gift from the Great Spirit to his people.' And the Chippeways say that this is how the gift of maize was given to their people.

The Indians who told the story were teaching two truths which we think of on Harvest Thanksgiving Sunday. The story spoke of a struggle and that reminds us that all the wonderful things on our tables day by day only come as the result of great effort. We remember the work of farmers struggling with the plough to break up the hard ground, sowing the seed from which the crops will come, and of the labour involved in harvesting. We remember too the struggle of people all over the world, in plantations, orchards and fields, so that we might be fed.

But the story also reminds us, as the Indian boy's father said,

23

that all the food by which we are nourished comes to us as the gift of the 'Great Spirit.' Without his good gifts of rain and warmth and sunshine, and the health and strength to do our work, there would be no crops.

So rightly today we are thankful for the hard work of others, and for God's blessing on their labour. Because of that struggle and blessing we have food on our tables.

PRAYER

Father, we praise you that you have blessed man's labour and given us again the wonderful gifts of the harvest. Help us never to forget that they are your gifts and so to be truly grateful. In Jesus' name.

Amen

Pirnmill

NOTE

This talk could be used as a sequel to 'KEEP YOUR EYE ON PAISLEY' on page 73.

VISUAL AID

An empty bobbin.

Pirnmill is a small village lying on the north west of the isle of Arran off the west coast of Scotland. Like many other villages, it has a school, a post office, a church and a number of houses. It is a particularly attractive village because of its position. Pirnmill faces the sea, so that nearly all the houses look over towards Carradale, in Kintyre, which is about seven miles across the water.

The village has an interesting history and its name gives a clue to what it was. The name is made up of two words. The second part is the word 'mill'. So Pirnmill must have had something to do with a mill. At one time, in fact, there was a mill in the village and the building still stands today even though it is no longer a workplace. In more recent years it was made into a house. The other part of the name is the word 'pirn', and that tells us the kind of work that the people did at the village mill, for 'pirn' is an old Scots word for a bobbin. So Pirnmill got its name because, a long time ago at the mill there, timber from a nearby wood was made into 'pirns', or bobbins, to carry thread.

From Arran, these were then shipped to the great mills of Paisley where the thread was made. Recently we were thinking about the mills of Paisley and of the prosperity they brought to the town. Paisley people are proud of that and rightly so! But the people of Pirnmill have a right to be proud of their past too, for their small industry helped the great mills of Paisley to operate.

Making thread is a great skill, but the product is so fine that it has to be specially packed. If you simply wind thread into a ball, it becomes tangled, and somehow from a tangled ball, you can never find where the thread begins! On the other hand, by winding thread around a wooden bobbin like this, it is kept untangled, straight and taut, and ready for use.

It is a great thought that the pirns of Pirnmill were necessary to the huge thread mills in Paisley, just as the mills of Paisley were necessary for the bobbin-makers of a small Arran village.

Big industries depend on little industries, and little businesses depend on big businesses. They need each other. St Paul once said something like that about the members of the church. He said that whether their abilities were great or small, they needed each other. Some members of the church at Corinth thought that what they could do was more important than what other members could do. Paul told them a story about the human body to show how wrong they were (see 1 Corinthians 12:14-27). He said that no member of the church could ever say to another, 'I don't need you,' or 'My work is more important than yours.' In the service of God we need each other and each others' skills. All are necessary if the church is to do its job properly. So whatever gift you have, and whether you think it small or great, it is needed for God's service in the church and in the world, and for the good of others who depend on what you can do, just as you depend on them for what they can do.

Things to do

Think of some big industries which depend on the work of smaller firms to help them.

Prayer

O God our Father, help us to appreciate the work that other people do for us. Remembering that we need each other, make us willing to use the gifts you have given us for the good of all. In Jesus' name.
Amen

THE LULLABY

TEXT: PROVERBS 6:20-21

My son, keep your father's commandment, and forsake not your mother's teaching. Bind them upon your heart always.

Golden slumbers, kiss your eyes
Smiles await you when you rise.
Sleep pretty baby, do not cry
And I will sing a lullaby.

I wonder if you have ever heard your mother sing your baby brother or baby sister to sleep, just as she probably sang you to sleep when you were a baby too. If you have heard her, do you know the word we use to describe these songs? You heard it in the last line of the song I read to you a moment ago—it is the word 'lullaby.'

'Lullaby' is a strange word and it has an interesting story behind it. As you no doubt know, the first man on earth, according to the Old Testament, was called Adam, and his wife was called Eve. But there is an old Jewish legend which says that Eve was Adam's second wife. Before Eve, he had another, whose name was Lillith. The saddest part of the story says that Lillith did not like children and that she killed all her own babies after they were born. Then she flew away from Adam and became a demon. In time, the Jews gave the name Lillith to an evil spirit, which, they believed, roamed the desert places seeking to harm children. That is why mothers would sing a little song to protect their children which contained the words 'Lilia Abi' which mean 'Lillith begone!' And from the words 'Lilia Abi', our word 'lullaby' came.

Doubtless when mothers today rock their babies to sleep and sing a gentle lullaby, they are quite unaware that it may have begun in olden times when mothers sought to protect their children from an evil spirit called Lillith.

Parents still try to protect their children, of course, and they do it not by singing lullabies but by giving good advice and wise guidance. Parents can do that because they are older and wiser, and they can see many dangers of which children are quite unaware.

Sometimes we think that mum and dad are fussing when they tell us 'Be careful when you cross the road' or 'Don't talk to strangers' or 'Be careful about the friends you make and the places you go.' But when parents say these things, they do so to protect us from evil and harm, and we should be ready to listen to their advice. A wise man wrote the words, 'My son, keep your father's commandment, and forsake not your mother's teaching. Bind them upon your heart always.'

P R A Y E R

Lord Jesus, we thank you for parents, friends and teachers who care for us, and for all those whose wise teaching is for our good. As you obeyed your earthly parents, give us a similar obedience, that, as we grow in stature and wisdom, we may also grow in the favour of God.

Amen

The Potsdam Guards

Visual Aid

A large toy wooden soldier, or a drawing of a soldier.

Text: 2 Timothy 2:3

. . . therefore endure hardness, as a good soldier of Jesus Christ.
(Authorised Version)

I imagine that you have all seen toy soldiers like this one—a brightly coloured figure standing to attention on parade. Not so many years ago, a set of toy soldiers would keep a boy amused for hours on end. Today, indeed, a set of lead soldiers which many boys would have had forty years ago, and which is still in good condition, may be worth hundreds of pounds to collectors.

Did you know that there was once a king who collected real live soldiers? His name was Frederick William of Prussia, and there were two things about his soldiers which were very unusual. First of all, his soldiers were all over seven feet tall. Second, they never went to war or joined in any battle. The king considered that they were far too precious for that, so they simply paraded up and down for the amusement and pleasure of the monarch. These soldiers were known as the Potsdam Guards, but they also had the name of 'blue boys' because of their bright blue uniforms.

To tell you the truth, the Potsdam Guards was not a particularly happy regiment. Discipline was harsh and desertion punishable by death. For that reason very few men volunteered to join the 'blue boys.' So to keep his regiment up to strength, Frederick William sent his agents all over Europe looking for men over seven feet tall, whom they could persuade, or even trick, into joining.

It is told how one very tall man, a carpenter to trade, was approached by an agent of the king and asked to make a box as long and as broad as the carpenter himself. When it was finished, the agent pretended to be unhappy with the result.

'It's not big enough,' he complained.

'Yes, it is,' replied the carpenter. 'I shall prove it to you.'

And with that he climbed into the box and stretched himself out full length. The agent then signalled to his helpers hiding near-by, and they quickly nailed the lid on the box, with the protesting carpenter now a prisoner inside. And so another recruit had been kidnapped and was on his way to join the Potsdam Guards.

By such methods, King Frederick William eventually collected a total of two thousand of these giant soldiers—soldiers who never went to war.

None of us would have been nearly tall enough to serve King Frederick William of Prussia, but thankfully none of us needs to be a giant to serve the King of Kings. Whether we are tall or short, we can all serve the Lord Jesus. Nor will he ever trick us into service where there is no real soldier's work to be done. Instead he asks for volunteers who will play their full part in the constant battle against evil. Will you be one of his army?

THINGS TO DO

1 Look up Ephesians 6:11-18 and discover the armour which the Christian soldier should wear.

PRAYER

Father, you give us all a call to serve and a task to do. Make us glad to follow and eager to fight cruelty and wrong. In Jesus' name.

Amen

THE MAN IN THE WALL

TEXT: EPHESIANS 4:26

Do not let the sun go down on your anger.

On the banks of the River Stour in the county of Dorset in the South of England, there stands a beautiful old church called Wimborne Minster. Among the many interesting things to be found in it, which include a chained library and an astronomical clock, there are the tombs of notable people who lived in the past. There is, for example, the tomb of a man called John Beaufort, Duke of Somerset, and his lady, Margaret. On the lid of the tomb there is, carved in alabaster, a full size figure of the Duke and his wife. They lie side by side, each clasping the other's right hand. Even though tombs may be sad places, there is something happy about the carving of a man and wife whose love for each other would not end with life itself.

There is one tomb, however, which is not only unusual, but in contrast to that of the Duke and his wife, speaks not of love but of resentment. It is the resting place of a man called Anthony Ettricke and it is known as 'the man in the wall.' Tradition says that he was rather eccentric and that somehow the people of Wimborne offended him. No one now knows why it happened or what was said or done to cause his resentment, but, whatever it was, Anthony Ettricke made a terrible vow. He decided that he would have nothing more to do with the people of the town, and that when he died, he would be buried neither in their church nor without it, neither in their ground nor above it.

As time passed on, however, he began to long that he could be buried with his ancestors. So, because he was unwilling to break the terrible vow he had made, he sought permission to be buried not inside the church, but inside the *wall* of the church. For that reason an alcove was cut into the church wall, and in the alcove—not in the church, nor without it, neither in their ground nor above it—he was buried in 1703.

All who visit Wimborne Minster learn the sad story of 'the man in the wall', Anthony Ettricke, who refused to forgive and forget his quarrel with the people of the town. But the story, in fact, is even sadder still, for Anthony Ettricke had expected to die in 1693, and he actually had that date inscribed on his tomb when it was prepared. He did not die, however, until 1703, and visitors can see that the original date on the tomb has been changed to the date on which he did die, ten years later. That means that Anthony Ettricke not only lived ten years longer than he expected, but that he had ten extra, precious years in which he could have healed his quarrel. Instead he nourished his resentment and kept his bitter vow to the last.

When he was writing to the Christian people in the church at Ephesus, Paul gave them some very wise advice. He said, 'Do not let the sun go down on your anger.' That is to say, we should never carry a quarrel into the next day, far less a lifetime. For all of us, each new day should be a new beginning in which we try to live in harmony with each other.

PRAYER

Lord, help us never to bear a grudge. Help us never to nourish resentment. Grant that we may be able to forgive, as you have forgiven us. In Jesus' name.

Amen

FEATHERS

VISUAL AIDS

A selection of birds' feathers including, if possible, a peacock's tail feather.

TEXT: PSALM 91:4

He shall cover thee with his feathers, and under his wings shalt thou trust.
(Authorised Version)

This morning, boys and girls, I am holding, behind my back, a collection of articles, all of the same type. Some of them are tiny. Some are quite big. Yet the whole lot put together weigh almost nothing at all. I wonder if you can guess what kind of collection it is? .... No? Well, I've already given you a clue by saying that the whole collection weighs almost nothing. Here is another. We often say that an object is 'as light as a . . . .' That's right! Light as a feather! And my collection this morning is a collection of feathers.

Just look at them, boys and girls. Feathers are truly remarkable things. They are so light and fine and delicate, and yet they are used to perform several tasks.

Their main purpose, of course, is to enable a bird to fly. The specially adapted wing and tail feathers are designed for that. They make it possible for the bird to 'take off' and, just as importantly, to land safely again. In the Tower of London there are a number of ravens. These big black birds are free to hop around

34

the grounds all day. The one thing which they cannot do, however, is fly away, because their wing feathers are deliberately trimmed.

But feathers serve another purpose. In the cold days of winter, a bird uses its feathers to help it keep warm. To do that the bird will fluff out its feathers, trapping air between them, and this acts as a kind of insulation.

Another thing that feathers are used for is protection. Birds which nest on the ground have feathers which are brown and dull, and markings which enable them to blend into the background. For that reason it is possible to pass by a bird nesting on the ground, without ever knowing that it is there.

Other birds, in contrast, have feathers of very bright colours—reds, blues and greens—like the peacock. Some people think that the peacock displays his bright colours to attract a mate, and others think that the 'eye pattern' of his feathers helps to frighten away enemies.

With all these uses, I am sure you will agree that feathers are wonderful things.

The Bible speaks about feathers. The Psalmist said, 'God shall cover you with his feathers, and under his wings shall you trust.'

The man who wrote these words did not mean that God actually had feathers. Perhaps he had seen a hen with her chicks, when suddenly an eagle or hawk had circled overhead, ready to swoop and snatch one of her young ones. And as he watched, he had seen the mother hen spread out her wings, while all the little chicks had huddled underneath for safety, staying there, until the danger was past.

The Psalmist was saying that our Heavenly Father will do the same for us. He is looking after us and, no matter the danger, he is always near, so that we do not need to be afraid.

That is more wonderful than feathers themselves.

THINGS TO DO

1 What is the largest bird you can think of? What is the smallest? Find out the wingspan of each.
2 List any animals which you know are protected by camouflage?
3 Isaiah once said that the man of or woman of faith is like a bird. Which bird was he speaking of? (See Isaiah 40:31.)

PRAYER

Father, many have found your presence to be a help and strength in time of trouble. Help us to live without fear, knowing that under your care we are secure.

Amen.

TALKING HANDS

VISUAL AID

A white glove. Colour the inside of the forefinger and thumb red, to form a mouth. Sew on two black buttons above the forefinger knuckle joint for eyes. You now have a simple glove puppet.

TEXT: LUKE 24:40

He showed them his hands.
(Authorised Version)

In the early days of television, there was a ventriloquist who frequently appeared on the screen. Unlike most ventriloquists, however, he did not use a dummy. Instead he would carefully put on a glove (*do this with the prepared glove*) and then he would let his hands do the talking. (*Do a small section of cross talk with the glove, allowing the children to share the idea.*)

That was only fun, boys and girls, but sometimes people do talk with their hands. Sometime, just quietly watch people having a conversation and pay attention to how often they use their hands to emphasise what they are saying. So, a hand, or two hands stretched out in front of us, means, 'Please give me.' Two hands stretched out sideways, palms upwards, can mean, 'I've got nothing.' One hand stretched out in front of us, fingers turned upwards, can mean, 'No!'

One group of people who regularly talk with their hands are the deaf, those who are unable to hear. Deafness is a sad handicap. How terrible to be unable to hear the sound of the sea or the wind, or laughter, or music, or the voices of our friends. Yet deaf people have a very clever way of hearing. They do it with their fingers and their hands.

In the New Testament we read of a pair of hands which tell a very moving story. They were the hands of Jesus.

On Good Friday the soldiers drove nails into his hands which fixed him to the cross. A few days later he appeared to his disciples in a room, and, so that they might recognise him, he showed them his hands. One of the disciples, a man called Thomas, was not there at the time, and when the others told him what had happened, he would not believe it. 'Unless I see the mark of the nails on his hands,' said Thomas, 'unless I put my finger into the place where the nails were—I will not believe it.' And the following Sunday, Jesus appeared to his disciples again, and he showed Thomas his hands, and so Thomas at last came to believe that Jesus had been raised from the dead.

Among the deaf people who speak with their hands, there is a sign for the name of Jesus. Here it is, and it reminds us of Thomas. (*Touch the palm of the left hand with the right forefinger, and then the palm of the left hand with the right forefinger. Then hold the hands out palm upwards.*)

The hands of Jesus proclaim a love so wonderful that human words are not adequate to express it. His hands tell us that he loved us so much that he was willing to die for our sins.

Today, boys and girls, many voices tell us that there is no God, or that, even if there is, he does not care. God doesn't care? The hands of Jesus tell us, just how much he cares for us all. (*Touch the palms once again, and then hold the hands upwards.*)

38

Things to do

Try to learn the signs which deaf people use with their fingers and hands for the alphabet.

Prayer

Father, we thank you for our hands and what they can do. Bless our hands and grant that they may be used to help and not to hurt, to delight and not to destroy. For Jesus' sake.

Amen

IT'S A HARD JOB!

VISUAL AID

The 'Situations Vacant' section from a quality newspaper. Paste inside the job description detailed in the story.

TEXT: PROVERBS 31:28

Her children rise up and call her blessed.

I wonder, boys and girls, if you have ever seen your dad studying the 'jobs' page in the newspaper? I thought we might try that this morning and see if any of the 'situations vacant' would be of interest to us.

Here is one worth looking at. (*Read out any advertisement which offers a very high salary.*) I wonder who would like that job? Who would like to earn . . . . pounds a year? That is a great deal of money to earn.

Here's another one, boys and girls. (*Read out an advertisement of a job which offers the opportunity to travel.*) Who would like that job, boys and girls? I think we would all like that kind of work. How wonderful it would be to travel and to see as many interesting places as possible.

But listen to this one, boys and girls. I wonder who would like to apply for this one? (*Read out the following which you have pasted into the paper*): 'General House duties, including cooking, cleaning, washing, ironing. 14-16 hour day. Seven days per week. Must be able to work through interruptions and to super-vise others less able.

'The applicant must be attractive, smartly dressed, as strong as a horse, never unwell, have a cheery manner and the ability to smile in all situations. Remuneration small. Few holidays. No pro-motion.'

Well, boys and girls, how many of you would be interested in a job like that? Nobody at all? Maybe that is not surprising. I doubt if many would want to work for these conditions.

Maybe it is only fair to tell you that this job was not really in the newspaper. It is one that I made up myself because it reminds me of somebody that we all know in our own homes. Who am I thinking about? Who does all these things in the advertisement? That's right. It's our own Mother.

Mother is the one who does the cooking and the cleaning, the washing and the ironing, who looks after us for all the hours of the day, and who never has a day off. Mother is the one who always has to be strong and cheery and smiling. Mother is the one who has few holidays, no promotion, and little pay for what she does.

Yet the wonderful thing, boys and girls, is that she does all of these things willingly, because she loves us.

Today on Mother's Day, it is right to remember all of that, to thank God for our Mother, and to show her how much we care in return. Then she will be like a mother of whom one of the old Testament writers said, 'Her children rise up and call her blessed.'

THINGS TO DO

1 Discuss what you have done to make Mother's Day special.
2 Make a list of the things that Mother does.
3 Think of things that could be done every day to make her workload easier.

MOTHER'S DAY

PRAYER

Father, on this day we thank you for all who surround us with love and care, and especially for our Mothers. Help us, by what we say and do, to let them know that their care and concern for us is appreciated.

Amen

A CHEER FOR JESUS

TEXT: MARK 11:9

Hosanna! Blessed is he who comes in the name of the Lord!

I wonder if you have ever given 'three cheers' at the end of a school football or basketball match? It is a sporting way to finish a game whether we have won or lost. The team captain usually leads it: 'Three cheers for St Anywhere,' he or she will say, naming the opposing team; and to his three cries of 'Hip, Hip,' we respond with 'Hooray!', the volume of the shout increasing each time.

I suppose when you think about it, these are strange words to use for our cheers. What have our hips to do with cheering? Where do the words come from?

In the Middle Ages, Christian knights in armour are said to have used a version of our cheer. The letters H I P are thought to have been a gradual change from an original cry of H E P. These were the initial letters of a Crusader battle-cry, '*Hierosolyma est Perdita*', meaning 'Jerusalem has fallen.'

The word 'hooray' could also be from another battle-cry, which comes from the word 'Huraj', which means 'to Paradise.' It is said to be the cry with which Slavonic warriors pursued their non-Christian enemy.

Who would have thought that when we shout our cheers of 'Hip Hip Hooray', we are repeating cries that may have been used in battle, hundreds of years ago!

Today on Palm Sunday we also repeat a cheer in church, and this one is older still.

43

PALM SUNDAY

There was a day in the life of Jesus when the disciples, the crowds and the children combined to gave him a special welcome. It was the day when he rode into Jerusalem to pay his last visit to the city. On that occasion the people had cut down branches from the Palm trees, waving them and scattering them on the ground as he rode along, and there were cries of 'Hosanna! Blessed is he who comes in the name of the Lord.' That word 'Hosanna' was a cheer. Its meaning is 'Save now.' The people and the children of Jerusalem were cheering and welcoming Jesus as a King to save them.

Today on Palm Sunday we remember that welcome. We remember too that Jesus came, not just as Jerusalem's Saviour, but as the Saviour of the world. And as we repeat the ancient cheer of 'Hosanna!'—'Save now!'—we welcome him as Saviour and as the King who is to reign in our hearts and lives.

PRAYER

Lord Jesus, today we remember that you entered the city of Jerusalem where you were to die. As the people welcomed you on that day, so help us even now to welcome you into our lives, that you may reign there as King.

Amen

THE TRUMPET

VISUAL AID

A Trumpet.

TEXT: PSALM 98:6

With trumpets and the sound of the horn, make a joyful noise before the King, the Lord.

I wonder who can tell me what kind of instrument I am holding in my hand? That's right. It's a trumpet. The trumpet is a wonderful instrument and its clear sound is often used to provide a jubilant, triumphant note on very important occasions. So, for example at a royal wedding, or at the coronation of a monarch, or on great ceremonial occasions, you will hear a fanfare of trumpets from the Royal trumpeters.

In the Bible we read of trumpets sounding too. They were used in the worship of the temple where their distinct sound could be heard, heralding the praise of God.

In actual fact, boys and girls, besides the trumpet here in my hand, there are lots of other trumpets in the church this morning. Can you see them? Well, if not, have a look at the flower vases. As you can see, our church is decorated with daffodils today, and the centre part of every daffodil is called 'the trumpet.' So, on this bright Easter morning, it is as though these little trumpets were helping to sound God's praise.

EASTER

I wish I could play the trumpet and sound a fanfare with this instrument in my hand at the moment, for Easter Sunday is the happiest day on the Christian calendar, and calls for all the jubilant, triumphant notes we can sound. On this day we rejoice because we remember that Jesus was raised to newness of life by the power of God our loving Father. This morning of all mornings we should be sounding a triumphant note.

Not long ago there lived a famous preacher called William Sangster. He used his voice to praise God in word and song, but sadly he became ill and gradually grew weaker and weaker. On the Easter Sunday, shortly before he died, he whispered to his daughter, 'It is a terrible thing on Easter morning to have no voice to praise the Lord. But it is an even more terrible thing to have a voice and *not* to praise him.'

Maybe, boys and girls, just like me, you cannot play the trumpet. But this morning, when the daffodils seem to be sounding their fanfare of praise to God, we have our voices. So let us use them to sound a great note of joy and triumph, as we remember and rejoice that Jesus is not dead, but alive for evermore.

PRAYER

Father, we raise our voices to swell the great note of praise which rises from all round the world today, as people in every land rejoice that Jesus lives. Help us not only to praise, but to follow him as our Guide and Friend.

Amen

THE LIGHT

VISUAL AID

A 'Magic' birthday cake candle of the type which re-ignites a few seconds after it has been blown out.

TEXT: JOHN 1:4

The light shines in the darkness, and the darkness has not overcome it.

One of the ways by which I know that Christmas is just around the corner, is when I see the presenters on the popular children's programme 'Blue Peter', bring out the Advent Crown and light the first of four candles. The lighting of candles has for a long time been a traditional part of the Christmas season. In Victorian times, when the Christmas tree became fashionable, people would place little candles on the branches—very dangerous, but no doubt very pretty.

John in his Gospel, when he tells of the birth of Jesus, says that a light came into the world. And Jesus himself said that he was the light of the world, and that, if we followed him, we would never walk in darkness.

At that first Christmas a light came into the world. Let's light a candle to celebrate that event. (*Light the 'Magic' candle.*)

But as you know, no sooner had Jesus been born than evil King Herod tried to put the baby to death. He sent soldiers to Bethlehem with orders to kill all the young children in that village. (*Blow out the candle. It should re-light within a few seconds.*) But the child was not there. His parents had taken him to a place of safety.

Then some thirty years later, others thought that they had finally succeeded in doing away with him. They crucified him and felt sure that that was the end of the matter. (*Blow out candle.*) But God raised Jesus and thus the light continued to shine.

Down through the centuries it has been the same story. Roman emperors, dictators and various governments have tried to blot out the Christian faith. They had Christians put in prison. Some were even put to death. (*Blow out candle.*) But always a few faithful people continued to love God and follow the teachings of Jesus, and thus the light continued to shine.

And so, over this Christmas season, whenever you look at the flame of a candle, or the lights on a Christmas tree, remember Jesus who is the light of the world and make it your resolve to keep the light of the Christian faith burning brightly.

PRAYER

Father, as we remember that Jesus came to be the light of the world, we thank you for all who through the ages have kept the light of faith burning so that the darkness has not been able to overcome it. Help us, in our day, so to walk in the light we see in Jesus, that others too may see their way to follow him.

Amen

THE FORGETTING HEAD

VISUAL AID

If possible, make a paper-maché head, bearing at least a slight resemblance to the speaker.

TEXT: PHILIPPIANS 3:14-15

. . . forgetting what lies behind and straining forward to what lies ahead, I press on towards the goal for the prize of the upward call of God in Christ Jesus.

Among the many characters created by the author Keith Water-house, none are more strange than those associated with Worzel Gummidge, the scarecrow who can walk about freely. There is Crow Man, for example, whom Worzel treats with great respect, calling him 'Your Most Worshipful Exaltedness', for it was Crow Man who put Worzel together. Another is Aunt Sally, a large wooden figure who is very cruel in what she says and does to Worzel. Yet he still loves her. Then, of course, there is Worzel himself, who is always involved in some adventure.

One of the most strange and wonderful things about Worzel is that he has a variety of heads; so that when he has some special job to do, he will put on the head for that particular task.

On one occasion Worzel had to go to a village dance, so he put on his 'dancing head.' To fight a duel with the local squire, he put on his 'fighting head.' In other stories he puts on his 'singing head' or his 'thinking head' or his 'remembering head.'

Perhaps it would be a good thing if we too could put on a

49

variety of heads. I have a spare head with me this morning. What kind of head shall we make it? We could make it anything we choose, but as we are at the end of a year and about to enter a new one, I suggest that we should call it a 'forgetting head.' As an old year ends, a 'forgetting head' could be a very useful thing, for there are things that we should all blot out of our memories. We should forget the mistakes we made, hopefully having learned a lesson from them. We should forget the angry words we spoke, and resolve never to utter such words again. We should forget the unkind things we did and decide to be more considerate in the future.

In the New Testament, we find these words written by St Paul: 'Forgetting what is behind me, I press on . . . .' Paul had not always been a follower of Jesus. There was a time when he had made it his business to arrest and punish those who were Christians. But the day came when his life was changed and he came to believe that Jesus was his Saviour and Friend. From that time on he did not waste his energy brooding over past mistakes. He put the past behind him. He forgot it and tried to serve God better each new day.

Just like St Paul, let us put on our forgetting head today, and, as the old year dies, press on into the New Year, doing our very best to serve God and to follow the example of our Lord Jesus.

THINGS TO DO

Make a paper maché head.

PRAYER

Father, there are things in the past that all of us want to forget—angry and bitter words, selfish and unkind actions. Help us to know that while we are capable of these things, you will support us in all our efforts to do better in the future. Then like your servant Paul, help us to go forward to better things, relying not on our own strength but on yours. In Jesus' name.   *Amen*

SAINT VALENTINE'S DAY

VISUAL AID

A card showing a heart with an arrow through it.

TEXT: ROMANS 5:8

But God shows his love for us in that while we were yet sinners Christ died for us.

On St Valentine's Day, we send cards to tell people that we love them. On the cards there is often a sign to show that we love them. Does anyone know what that sign is? The sign is a heart with an arrow through it. You can see it on this card which I have made. (*Display visual aid.*)

Some years ago, on a Radio Clyde programme, the DJ who is called Tiger Tim told a story of a disaster which occurred on St Valentine's Day. The 'Wee Arra People' went on strike, and because the 'Wee Arra People' went on strike, there was nobody to make the arrows to put on the cards through the hearts. That meant that people were unable to send a message to other people, telling them that they loved them.

It was only a story, of course, but what a disaster were such a thing to happen! I suppose it is just as sad when you don't get any Valentines. Maybe then you are left wondering if anybody does love you after all.

Christian people, however, know that there is someone who

51

loves them, more than anyone else ever could. That person is God. Jesus died on a cross to assure us that God loves us and forgives us, and then he rose from the dead to show that he is still with us, and still loves us and cares for us.

Christians have a sign just as St Valentine's Day has a sign. It reminds us of just how much God loves us. The sign is that of the cross itself. If there wasn't a cross, then we might not realise how much God loves us. The heart with the arrow through it tells us that somebody loves us on St Valentine's Day, but the cross tells us that God loves us every day and all the time.

THINGS TO DO

Go round the church and see how many crosses you can find in it. Note where you find them.

PRAYER

O God our Father, we thank you that in Jesus you have shown your love for us. We thank you that every time we see the cross in our church, we are reminded of just how much you love us. Help us to love other people, so that people may see that we are Christians, and learn to follow Jesus as well.

Amen

Don't get found out!

Text: Matthew 6:3

But when you give alms, do not let your left hand know what your right hand is doing.

In the town of Hamilton in Lanarkshire, there is a large building called the Mausoleum. It was built by the Dukes of Hamilton as a burial place, but it is now no longer used for that purpose. Over the years, because of the mine workings around Hamilton, the Mausoleum has sunk considerably, but it is still worth a visit, and inside there is a most wonderful echo.

On the huge doors there are figures carved in brass, and the guide to the Mausoleum proudly shows visitors that the carvings were made with the utmost care. The back of the heads of these figures are against the door so that it is impossible to see them, but the guide will take a mirror and, placing it behind, will show that the back of the heads is as carefully fashioned as the front which can be seen. This work was obviously done by someone who was just as anxious to make as good a job of what was not seen, as he was of work which everybody could see. After all, who was ever going to study the back of the heads of figures set against a door?

Sometimes people only worry about what is seen, and they are not too careful about the things that are not noticed. In Jesus' time, some people were very anxious that everyone should know when they were giving money to help other people. Indeed, they made sure of it by getting a servant to blow a trumpet at a

53

street corner to summon poor people to come and received money. This was done, Jesus said, so that everyone would see how kind they were, and he suggested that it was far better to give help in such a way that it would not be noticed. 'Let not your right hand know what your left hand is doing.'

Often boys and girls, and more especially men and women, are only worried about what people see. They worry about being 'found out' when they are doing something that is wrong, and they hate to think that if they are doing something that is good nobody knows anything about it, and they perhaps even boast about it.

There is a wonderful little booklet published by an organisation called Alcoholics Anonymous. It is called *Just for Today*. In it, it is suggested that just for today, 'I will do somebody a good turn and not get found out; if anybody knows of it, it will not count.' The man who carved the figures on the doors of the Mausoleum was not particularly anxious to be found out. Jesus tells us to help people quietly and not expect to be found out. Why not try this week to do a good turn to somebody in the way that Jesus suggests, without 'letting our right hand know what the left hand is doing.'

THINGS TO DO

Plan to do a good turn, and don't tell anyone about it.

PRAYER

Lord, help us to work as hard and play as fair in your sight alone, as if the whole world was watching us. This we ask for Jesus' sake.

Amen

54

THE LOST SHEEP

VISUAL AID

Have 99 sheep scattered around the church. (If cleaners and church officers have reservations about live sheep, it is possible to make sheep from cotton wool and pipe cleaners!) Keep one other extra sheep out of sight.

The children should be set the task of finding these sheep which have been placed fairly conspicuously.

When the children bring them up to the front, count the sheep in bundles of ten and have someone primed during the counting process to plant the hundredth sheep somewhere out of the church. When it is clear that one sheep is missing, ask the children whether it is worthwhile looking for the other one, or whether they should just make do with what they have. Eventually, when they decide to look for the lost one, and have retrieved it, read to them the story of Jesus in the following text.

TEXT: LUKE 15:4-6

Jesus believed that every single person is important. He believed that if a shepherd had a hundred sheep and one was missing, he would search all over the place to find it, just as you have done. Jesus cares for us as much as that. Jesus loves us so much that he is sad when anyone is lost or missing.

The love of God for all of us is just like that, like the shepherd looking for the one sheep, just as you have looked for and found our missing sheep in the church this morning.

THINGS TO DO

1 Find out the names of the different sheep which are bred in this country.
2 Draw a picture of a shepherd with a sheep on his shoulder.

PRAYER

God our Father, you are always looking after us as a shepherd cares for his sheep. Help us to know that you love each one of us, as if there was only one to love.

Amen

THE BIGGEST AND BEST WORD

VISUAL AIDS

A sheet with the word 'Smiles' written on it, and a sheet showing a smile like this

I wonder if anyone can tell me what the biggest word in the English language is? (*Listen to a few answers, or if none are forthcoming, one might suggest that there are big words like 'antidisestablishmentarianism', or the Mary Poppins word, 'supercalifragilisticexpialidocious'.*)

Yet, boys and girls, even these are not the biggest words in our language. The biggest word in our language has only six letters, and I have written it for you on this card. (*Display the card showing the word 'Smiles'.*)

Why is that the biggest word? Obviously, because there is a *mile* between the first letter and the last. Not only is it the biggest word, but it is also the *best* word, because when people have smiles you know that they are happy, and when people have a smiling face it helps to share that happiness with other people. Happiness is spread around by smiles.

Alice in Wonderland met a very special cat which always seemed to have a smile on its face. Do you know what kind of cat it was? It was a Cheshire cat. Not only did the Cheshire cat have a lovely smile on its face, and seem to grin all the time, but it could also disappear. And when the cat disappeared, it did so beginning at its tail, and then gradually continued to disappear bit by bit until its face disappeared, and then the smile disappeared last. Indeed, the smile remained sometime after the cat had gone. (*Show here the picture of the smile.*) It seems a strange idea, doesn't it—the smile remaining after the cat has gone—but isn't that quite often what happens with people who are happy? They leave you and you are still smiling.

Jesus' friends were always happy to be with him. As they went around with him, he gave them a peace and contentment which made them happy. At first, when he died, they were very sad because they saw him no more, but then they discovered that the happiness remained with them. Although Jesus had gone, the smile seemed to remain.

The happiness Jesus gives stays with us even when we cannot see him, and that happiness spreads to other people. Just as you are happy when you are with somebody that you love, so somebody once said of the early Christians, 'see how these Christians love one another.' That is to say, the happiness that came from being friends of Jesus remained, and it was infectious.

'Smiles' is the biggest and best word, because smiles can show the happiness we have from being friends of Jesus. Smiles are also the things that linger on, even when a person has gone.

THINGS TO DO

Draw, *in pencil*, happy faces with smiles. Then rub out the faces and leave the smiles.

PRAYER

Lord God, we thank you for smiles and laughter. Help us, by our happiness and by our smiles, to cheer those who are sad, and to share out happiness with the people we meet. We ask this for the sake of Jesus through whom we have our happiness and peace.

Amen

CHOICES

VISUAL AIDS

A can of Coke, a packet of crisps, a tube of smarties, a doll and a football.

TEXT: MATTHEW 13:44

The kingdom of heaven is like treasure hidden in a field, which a man found and covered up; then in his joy he goes and sells all that he has and buys that field.

If you have ever seen the TV programme, 'The Antiques Roadshow', you will have seen a great many things on display which may be worth quite a lot of money. It may be a painting which is worth thousands of pounds. It may be an old jug. It may be a piece of furniture or an old chair. People will pay a lot of money for something which they believe to be of value. Before you bought something like that, you would have to be sure of what it was worth, what its value was, before you named a price.

How much are these things worth to you? How much is a can of Coke, for instance? How much would you pay for this packet of crisps? What about the Smarties? Since you know their value, you would not pay a pound for a can of Coke, or for a packet of crisps, or for a tube of Smarties. If you were asked for a pound for any one of these things, you would know that none of them is worth that and therefore you would not pay that sort of money.

Sometimes you may have to choose between one of two things and therefore you have to decide which is of greater value to you. Which, for example, is worth more to you—this doll I am holding or this football? Not everyone would choose the same thing. Some things are worth more to you than they are to other people. Some things are worth a great deal to you.

A long time ago Joshua, the leader of the Jewish people, challenged his people to make a choice. He asked them to choose between worshipping the gods of the countries around them, or worshipping the one true God. He said to them, 'Choose today whom you will serve, but, as for me and my family, we will serve the Lord' (Joshua 24:14-15).

We all have to make choices in life. We all have to choose the things which we think are worth a lot to us, and are valuable to us. Jesus asks us to follow him, and many who have done so have found that following and obeying him is worth more than anything else in life. It is the most valuable thing that they have ever found.

Jesus told a story of a man who was digging in a field. As he dug he found buried treasure, left there from a long time ago by somebody who had never come back for it. He knew that if he bought the field, the treasure would be his. To him it was worth more than anything else he had, so he went and spent all his money to buy the field and own the treasure.

Following Jesus, being faithful to him, doing the things he wants us to do, is really worth more than anything else. Sometimes, though, we have to make a choice between following Jesus and doing something else. Let's always try to choose that which has the greatest value of all.

Things to do

1 Cut out pictures of adverts from papers or magazines with the prices blanked out, and get other people to guess how much they are worth.

Prayer

God our Father, we will have so many choices to make this week, often between what is right and what is wrong. Give us the wisdom to choose what will please you, for that is worth more than anything else in the world.

Amen

THE MEANING OF PRAYER

TEXT: LUKE 11:1

Lord, teach us to pray.

One day the people in a church got together to discuss the weather, as they often do in churches. What worried them was that it always seemed to rain at the wrong times, and they decided that, in their prayers, they would ask God to send rain at times that would be most suitable. Since it seemed a good idea, they then decided to choose the particular day of the coming week on which they wanted rain, and to ask the minister to pray for it in the church service.

Monday unfortunately was out, because quite a few of the ladies did their washing on that day. Some of them wanted to hang it out to dry. That meant that Monday had to be a nice dry day so that the washing would not get wet.

Tuesday seemed a good day, but some of the farmers in the church had arranged for a contractor to come along who would cut and bale their hay on that day. So it had to be dry for them.

On the Wednesday, some girls in the Sunday School were going to an outdoor pop concert, and they wanted it to be dry for that.

On Thursday the school football team was playing a match. The boys, of course, wanted it to be dry so that the field was not too muddy.

Friday seemed to suit most people, but the Property Convener of the church had arranged for some men to come and repair the church roof. They could not do that if it was raining, so he felt that it had to be dry on Friday.

On the Saturday some of the men in the congregation had arranged to play golf. Playing golf in the rain can be a miserable affair. So they wanted it dry for the Saturday.

That only left the Sunday, and the minister said that they must not have rain on Sunday. That would be a perfect excuse for people not to come to church.

In the end they were unable to agree on any day on which they could ask God to make it rain. Because of their particular plans, one person or another wanted it to be dry on every day of the week, and nobody wanted to spoil the plans of other people. So the people in that church realised that you really can't ask God to arrange things in that way. You can't really pray just for what you want. They also discovered, however, that prayer is about more than that. They discovered something about each other and what each person wanted. They discovered that what happened for other people is important, as well as what happened for themselves, and that our prayers must take account of that.

How wise the disciples were when they asked Jesus to teach them to pray. There is so much about prayer that we all need to learn. One of the lessons is the one that the members of that church learned. Prayer is not a way of getting something that we want. Prayer changes us. It helps us to see what *other people* want, and to know what God wants, not only for us but for others too.

PRAYER

Help us when we pray, Lord, to hear what you are saying to us, so that when we ask you, you will give us what we need, even if it is not what we want. In Jesus' name.

Amen

What a Little can do

Visual Aids

One five pence piece and perhaps a picture of a church.

Text: Mark 12:43

. . . this poor widow has put in more than all those who are contributing to the treasury.

How much money do you think it would take to build a church like the one we are in this morning, or even like the one in this picture? It costs a vast amount of money. It would take hundreds of thousands of pounds, perhaps even as much as a million.

Before and after the Second World War, the Church of Scotland was trying to build new churches wherever new houses were being built in this country. (*Perhaps reference can be made to a local church here.*) At the time a famous Church of Scotland minister, John White, was doing his best to raise money to build all these churches and he wrote to people for help. One of the letters which he wrote was to all the children of the Church. In the letter he told them that for three pennies they could buy a brick which would be used to build part of a church; or for ten pennies they could buy a stone. People responded to these letters and John White loved to tell the story of one small boy who wrote to him in these words:

Dear Dr White,
I hear you are needing money to build new churches. I am sending you two sixpences to build one . . . .

65

Two sixpences would now be the same as a five pence piece. The little boy hoped that with a five pence piece like this, Dr White would be able to build a church. John White read this letter to a friend who had already promised a thousand pounds: the man was so impressed with the little boy's letter that he said he would double his thousand pounds and make it two. The man's brother came into the room, and when he was told the story he said that he also would like to double what was promised. Between them they had now promised up to four thousand pounds! However, Dr White pointed out to the two brothers that the cost of building a new church would be five thousand pounds, and the brothers agreed that they would make it five thousand pounds between them! And so the little boy's sixpence—five new pence—built a church.

It is not how much we give that is important, but being willing to give. It's not how much we do for Jesus that is important, the thing that counts is doing your best. Jesus was once standing at the church door. There he saw people putting in their church offerings and some very rich people put in a lot of money. Then a woman passed and put in two of the smallest coins that could be given. She was very poor but Jesus said that she had given more than all the others because she had given everything that she had.

The widow's tiny coins were used by God every bit as much as the large sums of money which the rich people were putting in. The little boy's sixpence was used by God just as much as the thousands of pounds that the brothers gave. God uses even the little and does a lot with it. God is very happy to receive what we give when it is our best.

PRAYER

Lord, you made this world out of nothing. You can take even the little we have to offer and can use it. Accept us and all that we have, and use us in your service and to your glory

Amen

WHAT DO YOU SEE?

A sheet of paper with clock showing Roman numerals.

Many of you today will have watches of the digital type. Do you know why they are called 'digital' watches? It is because they have numbers on them, rather than the old kind of watch which had a face and hands. Some of the clocks in your house may still be of the type which have faces with hands and numbers on them.

Before these clock faces were used, however, many clock faces had a different kind of number, the sort of numbers that were used in the Roman Empire. If I showed you a clock face like that this morning, would you know whether I had put the numbers the right way up, or in the proper order, so that I have the correct numbers for 1, 2, 3, 4, 5, 6, 7, 8, 9, 10, 11, 12? (*Show your drawing, and, after a moment, put it down again.*)

Now, can you tell me, were the numbers on that clock face correct, or was there something wrong with them? (*After various responses have been given . . .*)—What I really want to know is, if you can tell me whether or not there were any hands on my clock? In fact, I want those who think that my clock had hands, to hold up their hands now. If you thought there were hands, what was the time on the clock?

You see, the problem is that I asked you to look at one certain thing, the numbers on the face. That is why many of you didn't see the hands, or the time they were pointing to. We often only see the things that we are looking for. I asked you to look for the numbers, and that is all that many of you saw!

The same thing is often true with people. We only see what we look for. Sometimes we look for good in people and we find it. Sometimes we don't look for good in people, and we don't find it.

When God was looking for someone to help him spread the Christian Church, he saw one man, Paul, in whom he thought there was a great deal of good. Nobody else did, however, because all that they could see about Paul was that he was hurting and harming the Church and the people who were Christians. God saw good in Paul, and he called him and used him (see Acts 9:10-16).

What you find depends on what you are looking for. If you look for good in people, then you will find it, but if you only look for the wrong things, then that is all that you will find.

THINGS TO DO

Try to make a clock face and put hands on it pointing to your favourite time.

PRAYER

Lord Jesus, help us to look for good things in people. And we ask you that you and others may forgive us for the wrong things that can be seen in us. Amen

68

THE BREAD OF LIFE

VISUAL AIDS

The letters B, R, E, A, D, which can be stuck individually on to a board or sheet of paper.

TEXT: JOHN 6:35

I am the bread of life.

I wonder, boys and girls, if you can solve a riddle. I am going to read you a poem, each line of which should give us a letter of the alphabet, so that by the time we come to the last line, we should have a word. (*The following poem can be read through whole, then repeated one line at a time, and the letters put up on the board as they are guessed*):

> *My first is an insect that lives in a hive.*
> *The second starts right, is in four but not five.*
> *The third is in ten and in nine, eight and seven.*
> *My fourth is the first of angels in heaven.*
> *My fifth is in dog but is not in cat.*
> *The whole word you eat though it can make you fat.*

What is the whole word, boys and girls? Yes, it is bread.

Perhaps nowadays you don't eat so much bread. You have lots of exciting things like chocolate bars or chocolate biscuits to take to school with you for your playtime piece. Or when you want something to eat when you are out playing, you might well ask for a bag of crisps. Quite a number of years ago, though, what a boy or girl would ask for, was a 'piece and jam'. Two bits of bread with nice jam in between was considered to be a great treat. That, for many boys and girls, was their playtime piece.

A Glasgow folk singer, remembering his schooldays in the city, before the multi-storey flats were built, told how the 'piece and jam' was sometimes thrown out of a tenement window to a child waiting below. Realising that this could no longer be done with ease or safety from a multi-storey, he wrote a song about it, 'You canna throw pieces from a twenty storey flat.' (*Here, if it is within the repertoire, scope and taste of the speaker and congregation, a short rendition could be given.*)

In some places, a long time ago, bread was the most important and sometimes the main part of a person's food. People needed bread to stay alive.

When the Jewish people escaped from Egypt and journeyed across the desert looking for a new land to live in, they were fed with bread in the desert. Without that they could not have survived.

Jesus once said to his friends, 'I am the bread of life'. What he was saying was, 'You can't have real life without me.' He said that he was the real bread, the true bread which everybody needs to have a perfectly happy and satisfying life.

PRAYER

We thank you, God, for the food that keeps us fit and gives us life. We ask you to give us also the strength and wholeness which comes from trusting you, and from following Jesus Christ as Lord and Saviour.

Amen

Choosing

TEXT: JOHN 15:16

You did not choose me, but I chose you.

The Jewish people wanted a king. So they went to Samuel and asked him to choose a king for them. Samuel did it in this way. He told the people to line up clan by clan, and from the clans he chose the tribe of Benjamin. Then he made the tribe of Benjamin line up family by family, and he picked the family of Matri. Then he asked the family of Matri to line up one by one, and from that family he chose Saul, the son of Kish (1 Samuel 10:17-24).

I wonder how *you* go about choosing people when you are selecting a team for a game. How do you make your choice? Some boys and girls recite choosing poems, pointing to a member of the group as each word of the poem is said, so that the person pointed out as the last word is said is selected for the team. Who would like to recite one of the choosing poems that you know? (*It is advisable to vet these poems beforehand as sometimes they can be obscene and an embarrassment to the parents whose children recite them!*)

When a team is being chosen, it's always nice to be chosen first, but it is not very nice to be left to the last. When that happens you see everyone else being picked, and you are standing there and nobody seems to want you or pick you.

When Jesus wanted to tell people about the love of God, he needed people to help him. He chose different people, not always of the kind we might have expected. He went along the seashore and chose fishermen, whereas the important people at the church doubtless thought that they should have been chosen first. Jesus once told his friends, 'You have not chosen me. I have chosen you.' Jesus doesn't leave anyone out. He chooses us, he wants us, he cares for us, and none of us ever need fell that we are left out, unchosen and unwanted. Jesus' love is for every person, and when he chooses, he chooses us all no matter what we are like. Jesus chooses us because he loves us and cares for us and wants us.

When you are chosen for a team, you do your very best for that team to help it win. Jesus chooses us for his team in the world, so we have to try and do our very best for him. We do that by having the same love for other people as he has for us, so showing them that Jesus loves *them* as well as *us*.

PRAYER

We thank you, Lord Jesus, that you have called us and chosen us to follow and serve you. Help us to try hard and play fair in this world because we are on your side, and because you love us and want us as we are. This we ask for Jesus' sake.

Amen

KEEP YOUR EYE ON PAISLEY

VISUAL AID

A bobbin of thread.

TEXT: HEBREWS 13:8

Jesus Christ is the same yesterday today and forever.

A long time ago a famous politician said, 'Keep your eye on Paisley.' A lot of people have been doing that every since. Indeed some people think that Paisley people are worth watching. Like Aberdonians they have a reputation for being thrifty. Some people have even gone so far as to say that Paisley people put more money into the bank after they have been on holiday than they take out before they go.

The prosperity of Paisley and Paisley people was partly built on thread—little wooden bobbins like this wrapped around with thread, each bobbin costing only a small amount of money. From Paisley, the largest town in Scotland, bobbins of thread were sent to countries all round the world.

It may hardly seem possible that thread could help to make a town. But that is how essential thread is. It is needed to sew dresses and suits, buttons and hooks, zips and hems. Like bread, with which it rhymes, thread is something essential for ordinary life.

Some time ago they started to knock down one of Paisley's most famous mills, the Ferguslie Mills. Then suddenly the demolition was stopped, as people began to realise what was happening. Even so, all that remains of Ferguslie Mill is a sad ruin where once there stood a great industry.

The disappearance of most of this famous thread mill shows that nothing lasts for ever, not even the great industries on which great towns have been built. In fact, the only really lasting thing is God's love in Christ: 'the same yesterday, today, and forever.'

Christ came into the world to bring us that love. Christ lived to tell us the good news of that love. Christ died to show us nothing can destroy that love. Christ rose from the dead to show us that God's love is with us always. God's love enriches us all.

THINGS TO DO

1 See how many different colours of thread you can find in your house.
2 Learn to sew your buttons on.
3 If there is a sewing machine at home, ask to see how it works.
4 Read Exodus 28:1-6

PRAYER

O God, our Father, we give thanks for daily work and those who do it, and we give thanks for your great work of love in Jesus Christ. Let your love go on working in our world and in our hearts to save us and to help us.

Amen

FERGIE

VISUAL AIDS

Football scarves of St Mirren, or Aberdeen, or Manchester United. A pair of binoculars or a zoom lens camera.

Say 'Fergie' to some people and they will immediately think of scarves like these, or rather the football teams whose colours these are. They are thinking of Alex Ferguson, who has at different times in his career been, among other things, manager of St Mirren, Aberdeen, and now Manchester United.

But there is another equally, if not more famous, 'Fergie': Her Royal Highness, the Duchess of York. When this Fergie was expecting her first baby, one of the reporters of Reuters, the famous news agency, spent more than twelve hours a day, for almost twelve days, up a ladder! He did so not to see the baby being born, or to find out the colour of its eyes or hair, but just so that he could see who went in and out each day to see the baby. He seemed to think the world would want to know.

Most of the people who visited were, as you might expect, family: the Royal Family. They are, like every family, very interested in every new addition to their number. Grannies and grandpas, brothers and sisters, uncles and aunts and cousins always love to see the new baby. Each new baby is special because it is family.

The Christian Church is often described as a family, the family of God. If this is so, then it is a strange family. Its members do not all know each other. They live in many different countries and speak many different languages. They even worship God sometimes in quite different ways. So what makes them a family?

75

The answer is God, their Father, and Jesus, his son. We are all related to each other through Christ. He shows us that God loves them and God loves us.

Sometimes this family is added to, just like Fergie's. In the Church we call this 'baptism'. At baptism a baby, or even an adult, becomes a member of God's Family—the Church. Through baptism God blesses them and shows again his love which makes them part of his family.

There is a well known evening hymn—'The Day Thou Gavest'— which tells how:

The voice of prayer is never silent
Nor dies the strain of praise away.

It tells us that the worship of God goes on around the world every minute of every day by God's family. Does it not give you a thrill to belong to a family as large as this?

THINGS TO DO

1 Make up your own family tree as far as you can.
2 Try to find out where missionaries of your own Church work as partners with other Christians, or where Christian Aid or the Tear Fund are helping people, and try to plot these countries on a blank world map.
3 Read the account of Jesus' family tree in Matthew 1.

PRAYER

We give thanks for our own families and for the Family of God in every land. Strengthen the Church in its work everywhere.

Amen

WALKING THE WAY

VISUAL AID

An ordnance survey map.

Do you like walking? Real walking? The kind of walking that Alfred Wainwright did? That kind of walking means that you have to use a map like this—an ordnance survey map. There is one of these maps for every part of Britain.

Alfred Wainwright became famous through walking. He was born in Blackburn in Lancashire. He left school at 13 and began work in the Burgh Engineer's Department in Blackburn local council. Later he transferred to the Burgh Treasurer's office. When he was a boy he used to go walking in the Lancashire hills. He described himself as being 'ill-shod and ill-clothed with jam butties in my pocket.'

One week in 1930 changed his life. He went for a holiday to Kendal in the Lake District and fell in love with it. After that he spent all his leisure time walking in that district. Eventually he transferred to the Burgh Treasurer's office in Kendal and lived there until he died in 1991.

On every walk, Wainwright kept a notebook with little maps and details of the routes he walked, the places to stop and see things, useful information on things of interest. People knew he was knowledgeable and he was always being asked for information. Finally he decided that the best thing to do was to publish his notebooks. They became his best-selling guides to the Lake District. He then even went on to write a guide to walks in the Scottish hills, which he also loved.

At the end of one of Wainwright's famous walks there is an inn. He decided to encourage people to make this particular walk, so he left some money at the inn. Each person who completed the walk was rewarded with a free pint of beer. So many people completed the journey that the reward was reduced to a half pint!

The Christian life is sometimes described as a journey and the Christian as a pilgrim, somebody who is walking with a purpose in mind. Jesus himself said to his disciples, 'Follow me' (Mark 1:16-18). He also said, 'I am the way' (John 14:6). That is our reward as Christians—to know that Jesus has walked before us on life's way, and to know that he will be with us in our walk of life, supporting us whatever the journey may bring, good or bad. If we want to know how to make this particular journey, we should always turn to him and to his example.

THINGS TO DO

1 Go to the local library and see if you can get a copy of one of Alfred Wainwright's guides to look at.
2 Learn how to set a map with a compass and find out what symbols are used on ordnance survey maps to describe things on journeys.
3 Read John Bunyan's famous poem about a pilgrim, 'To be a Pilgrim.' You will find it in the Church of Scotland Hymnary (Third Edition) as Hymn 443.

PRAYER

Lord Jesus, be with us every day of our walk in life. Cheer us when we are sad. Encourage us when we fall. Make us thankful when we succeed.   *Amen*

Up wi' the Bonnets!

Visual Aids

A number of bonnets and hats.

(*Try on some of the hats.*) Well, which one do you think suits me best? Not everybody looks good in a hat. Some hats do not seem to fit some faces. Other people wear hats as part of their uniforms, like soldiers and sailors, policemen and firemen, traffic wardens and postmen—even stockbrokers wear bowler hats!

David Livingstone, the great Scottish missionary who explored so much of Africa, is often portrayed wearing a hat. It had a little hard skip on the front and a cloth flap down the back to keep the sun off his neck. Livingstone was so attached to his hat that even when he came back to the less sunny climes of Scotland and England, he still wore his hat. He even went to a very important meeting of the Geographical Society in England among many distinguished people, still wearing his hat! Perhaps people thought he might need an operation to remove it!

After a while Livingstone returned to Africa. He went on journeying, but then no more was heard of him. His friends began to worry. 'Where's Livingstone?', people asked. 'Is he dead?' One of the great American newspapers sent one of its reporters to find him. His name was Henry Stanley. Stanley eventually found Livingstone, greeting him with the famous line: 'Dr Livingstone, I presume?' Since Livingstone had been ill and was resting from his journeys, Stanley stayed on with him for a while and the two men became firm friends.

At last, however, Stanley had to make his return to tell the world that he had found the great explorer. Livingstone wanted to give his friend a gift, but what could he give him? He had so little. But then, he had an idea. He took his most precious possession from his head and gave it to Stanley. It was his hat!

That is the sign of real generosity—to give to someone else something you hold precious and value yourself. God is generous like that. That is why he gave us Jesus. Jesus was his well-loved son. Jesus is God's precious gift to us and to the world.

That is also why, when we want to serve Jesus, we must give him from the things we value—our time, our money, our talents. Only what we value is good enough to give to him. Only our best is good enough for his services.

THINGS TO DO

1 Get a book on David Livingstone and read his story. Find out all about the wonderful journeys he made.
2 Make a scrapbook of people wearing hats and bonnets.
3 Read the story of Jesus on the Cross in any of the Gospels and find out what it cost him to love us.

PRAYER

We give thanks to you, O God our Father, for all those brave men and women who spread the good news of your love to every land. We pray now for the Church throughout the world. Strengthen its people that they may offer to you the best of their gifts for Jesus' sake.

Amen

SPELL OUT MY SOUL!

Some spelling cards.

TEXT: LUKE 9:23

... if any man would come after me, let him deny himself and take up his cross daily and follow me.

How good is your spelling? Can you spell 'Christmas'? (*Put up a flashcard with C R I S M U S.*) 'Knotted'? (*N O T E D*) 'Handkerchiefs'? (*H A N G E R S H I E F S*) 'Pictures'? (*P I C T O U R S*) 'Match'? (*M A C H*) 'Robbers'? (*R O B E R S*)

Well, did you get six out of six? Perhaps you think I am not very good at spelling? These cards do not show these words as I would spell them. They show how a little boy called Hugh Walpole spelt them. He was, as you will have seen, not very good at spelling.

Would it surprise you to learn that in his lifetime he became one of England's best known and wealthiest novelists. But he never did become a good speller. His secretary and his publisher had to correct his spelling.

What Hugh Walpole was best at was telling a good story. He had a great imagination. His books became bestsellers. What a pity it would have been if his lack of success at spelling had kept him from writing his novels.

A wayside pulpit once read, 'Success is never achieved by being afraid of difficulties.' Hugh Walpole overcame his difficulties with spelling. Jesus' disciples overcame their difficulties to spread the good news of God's love in the ancient world. Not even persecution, imprisonment, or the threat of death deterred them.

Jesus himself overcame the difficulty of the cross and rose again to proclaim his love for us. His overcoming we call the 'Resurrection'.

The Book of the Acts of the Apostles is full of stories of the difficulties Paul faced as he tried to spread God's word—earthquakes and shipwrecks, beatings and imprisonment, opposition and mockery. Paul found that being a Christian was not easy.

We will find the same. When we try to say the right thing and do the right thing, people can mock us. But we must remember 'Success is never achieved by being afraid of difficulties.' Like Jesus we sometimes have to take up the cross of cruelty and rejection (see Luke 9:23-27). If we want to spell out the good news of God's love to others, as well as to live up to its truth ourselves, we have to be prepared to be both persistent and courageous in our discipleship.

THINGS TO DO

1 Take your Bible and try to find some of those exciting accounts of Paul's difficulties in the Acts of the Apostles.
2 Read the story of Florence Nightingale, or William Wilberforce, or a modern person like Nelson Mandela. Find out what difficulties they had to face for the things in which they believed.

PRAYER

Lord Jesus Christ, you went on to do the Father's will in spite of the cruelty and hatred of men. Give us the courage to be faithful to you, and to do what we know to be right, even when to do it brings mockery and rejection. *Amen*

TREASURE IN HEAVEN

Do you have one of these? Most youngsters have. If you have a lot of money, they are no good. They are only for saving small sums of money. When they are full, the best thing to do is to take them to a real bank. You can usually find one in every town and city, or, if you live in the country, sometimes the bank will even come to you on wheels—a mobile bank.

There is one bank which is known as the Trustees Savings Bank (the TSB). It sometimes advertises itself as the bank which likes to say 'yes.' It was started by a minister. His name was Henry Duncan and before he was a minister, he was a banker in England. When he returned to Scotland and became the minister of Ruthwell near Dumfries, he started a bank for poor people. The other banks which existed then would only take a sixpence as the minimum amount of savings. Many could not afford that, but they could afford to put perhaps one penny per week into the large box in Henry Duncan's Savings Bank. If you ever visit Ruthwell, you can see the building that was his bank, as well as the box in which people put their money.

In the first four years of its existence Henry Duncan's Savings Bank collected £1160, a considerable sum of money for the early days of the nineteenth century. Each contributor had a little book in which the money saved was recorded. Every year that money earned some interest and so the savings grew. Soon, in many other places, savings banks were formed, until Parliament itself passed a bill to regulate them by law. Henry Duncan went all over Britain speaking on the subject to win Parliament's approval.

But Henry Duncan was not obsessed with money and wealth. He was the minister of Ruthwell for 47 years, his only parish. His parishioners loved him. When there was much unemployment locally, he ordered a shipload of wheat which was landed at Ruthwell creek to feed them. He gave the women flax to spin at their looms and the men seed potatoes to plant. He grew crops in his own manse glebe and gave the harvest to his predecessor's widow.

The only possible conclusion to make is that Henry Duncan learned from his Master, Jesus, that the only kind of treasures which are important are those treasures which are in heaven (see Matthew 6:19-21), and that it is more blessed to give than to receive (Acts 20:35).

Generosity is a great Christian virtue, especially when it is done not for thanks or reward, but just because a human need is seen and answered. Henry Duncan loved the people of Ruthwell and he loved them in really practical ways. This is how we are to love too. God has practical things for each of us to do for others so that we may express his love for them.

THINGS TO DO

1 Make a list of the major banks and find out all you can about them. The banks will often have some information available for young people to learn about their work.
2 Read the story of a farmer who paid too much attention to what he owned (see Luke 12:16-21).
3 Various charities, like the National Bible Society and the Leprosy Mission, have containers for saving small sums

of money for their work. You could use one of these, or a container of your own making, to save money for some good cause over a fixed period of time. Others might want to help you.

PRAYER

We thank you, God, for the work which gives the money that makes us able to buy food and clothes. Help us to see that there are some things money cannot buy, like the love of our family and parents, and your love in Jesus.

Amen

THE GREAT GRUMBLER

A picture of a camel.

If you ever see a creature like this and want to know whether it is a camel, there is an easy way to find out. Put a bundle on its back for it to carry. If it grumbles, it *is* a camel.

Camels grumble every time their driver loads them up for a journey, no matter how small the bundle. As every other bundle goes on, they keep on grumbling. It is as if they are saying, 'Do you expect me to carry that? I cannot possibly carry another thing. Remember I'm a camel and not an elephant!'

All the time this grumbling is going on, the driver takes no notice, but whenever the grumbling stops, the driver stops loading his camel. He knows that the next bundle might be 'the last straw that broke the camel's back.'

Jesus once told a story of two sons (Matthew 21:28-32). Their father asked each of them to go and work in his vineyard. One son grumbled and said no, but later he went and worked there. The other son readily agreed, but he never went near the vineyard. Jesus asked some listeners which of these two sons did what his father wanted. The answer, of course, was easy: the grumbler, the son who muttered but went. Jesus always said it is by what people do, not by what they say, that they should be judged.

If camels were to be judged by the grumbling they do, you might think that they would carry nothing anywhere. In fact they are great beasts of burden and will carry heavy loads over many miles and through very difficult terrain. Their grumbling and grunting is just their little way.

But of course it is better not to be a grumbler, especially when we are doing things for God and for other people. God loves those who cheerfully and willingly give their service to him. No one likes a person who does things for them grudgingly. Perhaps it is a good idea to be like the dwarfs in *Snow White* and 'whistle while we work.'

THINGS TO DO

1 Find out what you can about camels. Find out what kind of special camel a 'dromedary' is.
2 Make a list of the things people do about your church to help in its work.
3 Read these Bible passages in which camels are mentioned: Genesis 24, Isaiah 30:1-7, Mark 1:1-8 and Matthew 19:23-26.

PRAYER

Teach us good Lord to serve you as you deserve, to give and not to count the cost, to fight and not to heed the wounds, to strive and not to seek for rest, to labour and not to ask for any reward save that of knowing that we do your will.

Ignatius Loyola

SHAPES

Shapes of triangles, circles, rectangles and squares. The shape of a church spire, a cylinder, a tower with a rampart, and a cross.

Are you good at shapes? What are these shapes? (*Use the first set of shapes for a quiz.*) Shapes are important. We often recognise things by their shape: the bus coming in the distance, a Rolls Royce compared to a Metro, a sheep from a cow.

Churches too have different shapes. In England there are a wide variety of churches with different shapes. Some have a spire like this on the top of the building. (*Show shape of church spire.*) Churches do not need to have a spire, but men built them like that to point people looking at the church towards heaven and God. Lincoln Cathedral, one of England's finest cathedrals, used to have three spires, but they became unsafe and had to be taken down. People in Lincoln rioted, but eventually they had to agree with the decision because they simply did not have the money to replace the spires.

Some churches have a tower that looks very like a bit of a castle battlement. (*Show shape of tower with rampart.*) These towers look strong and remind people looking at the church that God is their refuge and their strength (Psalm 46). Long ago, if someone was fleeing for his life, he or she could claim sanctuary in a church. This gave the fugitive a number of days to avoid capture and to pray and think about the future. It also gave the pursuers time to

88

think whether they really wanted to capture the fugitive in the first place.

This kind of shape (*show the cylinder shape*) is rarer, but some churches have towers like this, especially in the eastern and flatter counties of England. They look more like watchtowers from which people could see far and near: perhaps to espie an enemy approaching in the distance, or to watch for ships at sea. Remember that Jesus told his disciples that they must be watchful (see Luke 12:35-40).

Whatever the shape of churches on the outside, this is generally the shape of churches on the inside. (*Show shape of cross.*) The cross is the shape which reminds all who worship God of his love which is shown to us by Jesus's death on the cross.

THINGS TO DO

1 Try to get some pictures of churches in your own area and put them into a book. Try also to find out what you can about their history.
2 The early Church had no churches. Read the Acts of the Apostles about the Church meeting in someone's house, and about the boy who fell asleep during Paul's preaching! (See Acts 20:9-12).

PRAYER

We thank you, God, for those who built our church and all who have worshipped here in times past. Help us to be the Church in our time, loving and serving you. In Jesus' name.

Amen

THANK GOD FOR WRITERS

VISUAL AIDS

A bottle of ink, some blotting paper, a fountain pen and a biro.

TEXT: PSALM 119:162

I rejoice at thy word like one who finds great spoil.

Here is a simple test to know whether people are over fifty years of age! Ask them if they know this rhyme:

They come as a boon and a blessing to men,
The Pipwick, the Owl, and the Waverley Pen.

These are the words of a once famous advertisement for this kind of pen—a fountain pen.

You have to fill this pen (*hold up pen*) from a bottle of ink like this one (*hold up ink bottle*), and every word it writes has either to be left to dry carefully or else you must blot it with this kind of paper, blotting paper (*hold up paper*). Important documents are usually signed with a fountain pen because the ink is longer lasting and does not fade easily.

But most of us prefer to use this kind of pen, the biro. It was invented by Lazlo Josef Biro, who was born in Hungary in 1899 and who died in Argentina in 1985, aged 85 years. He was only 17 when he invented a hand-operated clothes washer. Later he invented a pick-proof lock. But the invention that made his name famous was this pen. We simply call it by his name—the biro. It is a pen which is free from mess and which writes freely with ink which dries instantly. Biro certainly made writing easier.

Writing is one of the most important skills we learn. It makes it possible for us to give information and to gain knowledge, to thank people or even to express our love for them, to keep in touch with people even though they may be far away from us. Great writers use their skills to entertain and delight people.

The people who wrote the Bible, the book on which we think especially this Sunday, did not have fountain pens nor biros. They wrote with a very crude writing instrument called a 'stylus'. But thank God that they knew how to write and did write! Thanks to them we can read the good news of God's love for us. Thanks to them we can read the psalms of the Old Testament, the words of Jesus and the letters of Paul. Their writing is one of God's greatest gifts to us, and rightly today we give thanks for it.

THINGS TO DO

1 See what kinds of pen you have in your house and compare how they write.
2 Think of any other thing which we call by the name of the person who invented it.
3 Read Philemon, the shortest letter of Paul, and find out why he wrote it.

PRAYER

We thank you God for the gift of writing, for birthday and Christmas cards, letters of thanks and letters of comfort, but most of all we thank you for the Bible and for Jesus, the word of love that it contains.

Amen

CHRISTMAS DREAMS

VISUAL AID

A teacloth.

The minister could not sleep very well. He kept on tossing and turning in his bed. He had been at so many Christmas parties. He was full of mincemeat pies, Christmas pudding and turkey. He began to have the strangest dreams.

He was a housewife with a teacloth in her hands. The housewife was singing:

> *I am busy, you can see, for our Christmas Party*
> *All the family come to me and they eat most hearty.*
> *Chicken, turkey, ham and meat, mincemeat pies and jellies*
> *Everything that I can make to fill up all their WE-ELL-IES!*
>   (*Tune:* 'Good King Wenceslas')

The minister shuddered in his sleep and turned over again, but his dreaming did not stop. He was a shopkeeper now in a large department store, confronted by a mass of Christmas shoppers. He was singing under his breadth:

> *Here they are again this year,*
> *Again this year, again this year,*
> *Here they are again this year*
> *Desperate to spend their money!*

Perfumes, hankies, soap and ties,
Soap and ties, soap and ties,
Perfumes, hankies, soap and ties
For mummies and daddies and aunties!

My feet are killing. I wish they'd go,
I wish they'd go. I wish they'd go,
My feet are killing. I wish they'd go
So I can go home to the telly!

(*Tune* : 'I Saw Three Ships')

The minister woke up, rose from his bed and made a cup of tea. He returned to bed and tried again to get to sleep. He began yet again to dream. Now he was a head teacher, but he was singing.

God rest ye merry gentlemen
Let nothing you dismay.
I'll be glad to see the back of them
Upon this final day!
For pantos, discos, all have told
They've stole my strength away,
But thank goodness I'm going home to rest, home to rest
Thank goodness now I'm going home to rest!

(*Tune*: 'God Rest Ye Merry Gentlemen')

The minster woke again with a start. 'Yes,' he thought, 'Some people *do* think that is what Christmas is about—eating food, buying presents, always being in the party mood. But it is not. It is about the birth of Jesus, the happiness of a family, the joy of the angels, the curiosity of the shepherds, the devotion of the wise men, the coming of God to his world. He went back to sleep and slept more soundly.

CHRISTMAS

THINGS TO DO

1 See if you can make up some silly rhymes yourself about the things people do at Christmas.
2 Make a list of your favourite Christmas hymns and put down your favourite verse from each.
3 Pray for some of the people in the world that will have very little at Christmas, and think of any practical way that you and your friends could help them.

PRAYER

Our Father God, help us to remember why you sent Jesus into the world. Help our Christmas not to be selfish, but filled with joy at his coming, and with love to others.

Amen

TRJE CASSYN

A drawing of the Isle of Man coat of arms.

TEXT: EPHESIANS 6:11

Put on the whole armour of God.

Set in the Irish Sea, about half way between England and Ireland, is the Isle of Man. It has a most interesting history and a fascinating coat of arms. No doubt you have all seen it. It is called 'Trje Cassyn' or 'Three Legs.'

You will notice that it consists of three legs clad in armour, bent at the knee, and all joined together at the thigh, while one foot is directed skywards. The figure is surrounded by a garter in which are the Latin words '*Quocunque Jaceris Stabit*,' which mean: 'Whichever way you throw me, I shall stand.'

It is thought that this symbol was originally found on the coins of the Norse-Irish kings, some of whom once ruled in Man, and that later it came to be used on the island's official coat of arms.

Think about those words—'*Whichever way you throw me, I shall stand.*' In other words, it is impossible to bowl me over—nothing can knock me off balance. I wonder whether you and I could say the same thing?

Notice that the three legs are clad in armour. The Bible says that if we are to stand firm against all the evil things which threaten to overcome us, then we too need armour, and that God will

95

provide us with all the armour we need. We sometimes sing a hymn which talks about this:

Soldiers of Christ arise
And put your armour on,
Strong in the strength which God supplies
Through his eternal Son.

What is this armour? St Paul tells us in his letter to the Church at Ephesus. There is the belt of truth; the breastplate of righteousness; the Gospel of peace as shoes to provide a firm footing; the shield of faith; the helmet of salvation; and a sword which is the Word of God.

But armour alone is not enough. If we are not to fall in the battle against evil, there is something else we must do: that is why St Paul gives us a further piece of advice. For when we have put on all the armour he mentions, we must remember to keep praying.

Then we shall not fall, even when things are at their worst. Instead, we shall be able to stand and nothing will 'throw' us.

THINGS TO DO

1 Find the Isle of Man on the map. Can you name its capital?
2 Try to design your own coat of arms, or shield. Think of a suitable motto to add to it.
3 Find and write out a Bible verse about standing firm (see 1 Corinthians 16:13).

PRAYER

Heavenly Father, help us in the fight against the evil things which would overwhelm us, and grant that clad in your heavenly armour, and strengthened by prayer, we may be able to stand firm through all the storms of life.   *Amen*

Things Great and Small

Happy is he whose help is the God of Jacob, whose hope is in the Lord his God, who made heaven and earth, the sea, and all that is in them.

Have you ever noticed that people seem to be fascinated by things which are extremely big? The strange thing is that they seem to get equally excited about anything which is very, very small.

Perhaps you have been to a safari-park and gazed in wonder at a huge African elephant. You may have been told that it can weigh up to ten tonnes and that it can lift a full grown man as easily as you can lift your pencil. You gasp in surprise—as well you might.

You would be even more astonished if you could slip back in time some seventy million years ago to the age of the dinosaurs. Long before men came on the scene, the earth was inhabited by giant reptiles. No doubt you have seen pictures of them. One of the biggest—Tyrannosaurus Rex—stood six metres high and measured as much as fifteen metres in length. We know this from pieces of bone which have been found and fitted together by naturalists.

There are also many non-living things, *inanimate* objects, in God's creation which are so huge that they take our breath away. Consider an enormous mountain range, or the vastness of the ocean. Think of a giant tropical rainforest with its tall trees pushing their way skywards in search of sunlight.

Now, in contrast, turn your mind to something which is very small. Few people can resist the appeal of a tiny new-born baby. They gaze in wonder and admiration at the infant—so small and yet so perfectly formed. And in the world of nature we can find something even smaller. Ants, for instance, which lead such busy and organised lives, are so small that half a dozen of them could crawl about on your thumbnail.

By using a microscope it is possible to study forms of life which are too small to be seen by the naked eye. These life-forms are known as micro-organisms or microbes. Some of them are responsible for causing disease, but most of them are harmless and some are even helpful to man.

You can see giant reptiles, or at least their skeletons, if you visit the Natural History Museum in London. But if this is not possible, you can see life-size models of dinosaurs if you visit a Dinosaur Park. There is one in Colwyn Bay in North Wales, and another in Blackgang Chine on the Isle of Wight. Perhaps you know of others.

On the other hand, if the wonders of the microscope appeal to you more, you may like to know that in Buxton, Derbyshire, there is a Micrarium. There, by operating simple knobs and joy-sticks, you can enter into a world of tiny things. It is possible to see the various stages in the life-cycle of a mosquito, or to watch crystals melt and re-form in a blaze of colour and patterns which will amaze you.

To study the world of nature is to be filled with awe and wonder. This wonder leads on to worship, as we give praise and thanks to God who is the creator of all things.

Surely we must agree with the Psalmist of old who declared: 'Happy is he whose help is the God of Jacob, whose hope is in the Lord his God, who made heaven and earth, the sea, and all that is in them.'

THINGS TO DO

1 Try to visit a Natural History Museum, a Dinosaur Park or a Micrarium.
2 Make two lists—one naming some very big things and the other listing very small things.
3 Look at something under a microscope, or through a magnifying glass.

PRAYER

We praise you, O God, for the wonderful world you have created. Help us to play our part in looking after the planet which you have entrusted to man's care.

Amen

HALF A CLOAK

TEXT: MATTHEW 25:45

. . . as you did it to one of the least of these my brethren, you did it to me.

In London, near Trafalgar Square, stands the Church of St Martin-in-the-Fields. When it was built, it was surrounded by green fields, but now buses and taxis rush past its doors all day long. Many people come from far away to visit this famous church. Some come to worship. Others come because they have heard of the good work which is done there. And the poor and homeless know that they can find food and shelter and friendship. But who was the St Martin who gave his name to this famous church?

He lived hundreds of years ago in a country that belonged to the great Roman Empire. As a small boy he had watched the Roman soldiers marching along the street, their helmets gleaming in the sunlight, and he knew that when he was old enough he too would be a soldier. As soon as that day came, he enlisted. By this time he was already a follower of Jesus Christ.

He quickly adapted to the rough life of a soldier and was well liked by his comrades, although they did think that he was a bit odd. For Martin did things which they would not dream of doing. He actually stopped in the street and talked to beggars. And not only that, he gave them money. He seemed to have a deep love for people who were poor and homeless and lonely and he wanted to do all that he could to help them.

One day he came upon an old man sitting begging by the roadside. Martin had nothing to give. His wallet was empty! He noticed that the old man was shivering with cold. And then he thought of his own bright warm cloak and he knew what to do. He drew his sword and cut the large cloak right down the middle. With a smile he draped one half around the beggar's shoulders and the other half around himself. His friends teased him for being so foolish as to spoil a perfectly good cloak.

That night, as Martin slept, he saw Jesus in his dream, surrounded by the Heavenly Host. To his great surprise, the Saviour was wearing a brightly coloured piece of cloth over one shoulder. The Lord said, 'Martin, my good soldier, gave me this.'

Then Martin remembered that Jesus once said, 'as you did it to one of the least of these my brethren, you did it to me.'

Martin never forgot about that dream and later on, after he had left the Roman Army, he devoted his time to telling other people the Good News of Jesus. Many of these people had never heard of the Saviour before.

The church in the heart of London which bears Martin's name is surrounded by many reminders of this story. In the streets around the church, on the lamp-standards, there is a little picture in metal of a brave soldier sharing his cloak with a beggar.

THINGS TO DO

1 Draw and colour a picture to illustrate the story.
2 If you go to London, try to visit the Church of St Martin-in-the-Fields. Look out for the pictures on the lamp-posts.
3 Discuss (or write) what you think Martin would have said when his friends teased him for spoiling his good cloak.

PRAYER

Heavenly Father, we pray for all who are poor, for those who are homeless, for those who have no work, for those who have lost hope. Show us some way in which we can help them and help us to remember that in ministering to their needs, we are serving you. Amen

THE BOY BISHOP

TEXT: MARK 10:13

Let the children come to me.

Saint Nicholas has long been regarded as the Patron Saint of children and his special day is December 6th. On this date each year it was the custom in the Medieval Church, for a boy, chosen from amongst the choristers, to be enthroned as bishop. He held this office until Holy Innocents' Day—December 28th.

The boy selected for the honour was enthroned with due solemnity and dressed in robes befitting his high office. Should a boy bishop die during the short period he held office, it was laid down that he had to be buried with all the pomp and ceremony which would have been due to a real bishop.

During the reign of Elizabeth I the ceremony was abolished in England, but many years later it was revived and continued to be held in numerous places until quite recently. Berden in Essex was one such place. There the Revd H K Hudson, who was vicar of St Nicholas Parish Church from 1899 to 1937, not only brought back the delightful ceremony, but added new meaning to it.

Instead of serving for just three weeks, the boy bishop now remained in office for the whole year. During this time he was regarded as head of the Sunday School and leader of the young people in his village. He was expected to behave in such a way as to set a good example in all he did.

A play depicting events from the life of St Nicholas was written by the Reverend H K Hudson, and this was performed by the children of the village each year as part of the enthronement

102

ceremony. The part of St Nicholas was, of course, played by the boy bishop.

With the outbreak of the Great War, the custom of enthroning a boy bishop died out in Berden, and, unfortunately, attempts to revive it after the War did not succeed. There is, nevertheless, a permanent reminder of the historic ceremony in Salisbury Cathedral where visitors can see a unique sculpture of a boy bishop in full regalia.

Jesus spoke about the meek and lowly being exalted. He also had a special regard for children. The enthronement of the boy bishop reminds us of both of these things.

Do you remember the story of the mothers who brought their children to Jesus so that he could bless them? The disciples were displeased and tried to send them away, but when Jesus saw what was happening, he said, 'Let the little children come to me.' Then he placed his hands on them and blessed them.

Jesus had a special regard for children. He still has—for you.

THINGS TO DO

1 If you get a chance, visit Salisbury Cathedral and see the effigy of the boy bishop.
2 Look up Matthew 5 verse 5 and find our what Jesus said about the meek and lowly.
3 The following articles are associated with the office of a bishop. Can you say what each one is and what its use is? (a) *Cope* (b) *Crosier* (c) *Mitre*?

PRAYER

Lord Jesus, we thank you that you welcomed children long ago and that you are still calling children to come to you today, Help us to respond to you by yielding our lives to your service.

Amen

103

FLAGS AND BANNERS

TEXT: PSALM 20:5

. . . in the name of our God set up our banners.

If you were asked the question 'What is a flag?', you might well describe it as a piece of gaily-coloured material often attached to a flagpole. And yet we all know that a flag is much more than that. It is a symbol. It stands for something. Every country has its own distinctive flag; and organisations such as the Red Cross and the United Nations have flags too.

The flag with which you are most familiar is no doubt the flag of the United Kingdom—the Union Jack. It flies proudly over public buildings on special occasions such as the Queen's birthday. It flutters over the Houses of Parliament when the House is in session. But did you know that the Union Jack is really a combination of three flags? It includes the crosses of St George (England), St Andrew (Scotland) and St Patrick (Ireland).

Some individuals, kings and queens for example, have their own special flag. When the Royal Standard flies outside Buckingham Palace, we know that Her Majesty the Queen is in residence. A smaller version of her personal flag is displayed on the front of her car on ceremonial occasions.

From very early times, flags have been raised high on poles and carried into battle. The Roman legions had an eagle as their emblem and the flag was the rallying-point for the soldiers. So much importance was attached to the flag, that if the standard-bearer fell, another soldier was immediately ordered to replace him.

104

Most modern flags are rectangular, but in the Middle Ages flags of different shapes were quite common. Some of these were known as *pennons* and others were called *gonfalons*.

Many flags are quite simple in design, but others are more detailed. The flag of the United States of America is known as the 'Stars and Stripes.' It has 13 stripes representing the 13 original colonies and 50 stars for the 50 states of the present day.

Flags may carry religious symbols. An example of this can be seen in the crescent moon which some Muslim countries feature on their flags. Israel's flag has the Star of David at its centre.

Flags may help to identify ships at sea: for example, if a vessel flies a yellow flag it means that there is disease on board. Flags flown at half-mast on land or sea are a sign of mourning. A red flag means danger and everyone understands that a white flag is a token of surrender. Flags may also be used to send messages. This method of communication is known as Semaphore.

A banner is similar to a flag, but usually takes the form of a long strip of material stretched between two poles. It often carries symbols or slogans and can be seen on marches or in processions. If your town has an annual carnival you will certainly have seen plenty of banners representing the different groups and organisations taking part.

The Bible has something to say on the subject too. When the Israelites left Egypt and began to make their way towards the Promised Land, we are told that each tribe camped under its own banner as Moses had commanded (see Numbers 2:34).

The Old Testament Psalmist, in a service used in the temple, urged the people of Israel to 'set up their banners in the name of God.' At that point in the service, the banner-bearers would wave the banners they held in their hands.

It is a great thought that we can all 'set up a banner in the name of God.' To do this we do not actually need to carry a banner in our hands, but by the way we live we can show that we are on the Lord's side, that we are the people of God. If you and I try to live in such a way, I wonder if other people will recognise that we are God's people, and that we serve under his banner?

THINGS TO DO

1 Imagine an explorer has discovered a new country. It does not have a flag yet. See if you can design one.
2 What do you think might be the marks of those who serve under the banner of God? Perhaps you might discuss this.

PRAYER

Help us to show our allegiance to Christ by rallying around his banner, so that the world might know that we are on the Lord's side and in the service of the King.

Amen

PART 2

SCHOOL WORSHIP

CHURCH AND SCHOOL

The earlier part of this book has been concerned with relating worship to children within the church morning service. While it is hoped that children will learn from the stories and experience, the emphasis is upon inspiring attitudes and actions. The underlying assumption is that the ethos and community of the church, through regularity of attendance, will reinforce and support Christian motivated attitudes and actions.

School presents a very different scenario. The school community will reflect many different belief stances: various forms of Christianity, together with non-religious stances such as Humanism or Agnosticism, also devoutedly held religious beliefs of world religions such as Islam, Hinduism and Sikhism. In urban areas there will also be a large proportion of pupils who are, in reality, 'non-religious', having no meaningful experience or relationship with any form of religion. Being challenged, such pupils may reply that they are 'Christian', meaning that they are not Hindus or Sikhs or whatever, or possibly (and more likely) that they are Protestant or Catholic because distinct family roots so determine. The broad spectrum of the school is reflected in both staff and pupils, and, insofar as, for the latter, school acts *in loco parentis*, the stance of parents has to be respected whatever that stance is, whether religious or otherwise, regarding their children.

This rich diversity affords at once an opportunity for worship, but also a constraint. The foundation of church worship is the common sharing of a commonly-held faith, or interest in that faith, if it is not yet fully shared. The school offers no such common ground. The constraint is that the diversity of the school community must be respected. The opportunity is that, in Scotland, Chaplains are invited into schools to share their Christian faith and express their Christian worship.

WORSHIP:
CONSTRAINT AND OPPORTUNITY

Can we bridge the paradox of constraint and opportunity? Some considerations may help.

First is the awareness that for many the experience of worship provided within the school may be the only experience that many pupils, and indeed staff, may have. What is possible for a diverse community is to create a threshold of worship, an open door, through which all may see and feel what is happening; but as individuals to determine for themselves whether they choose to go through and how far they are prepared to share.

This threshold falls short of the clarion call of the Church: 'Let us worship God', but nonetheless it may be the first step on the road of initiation which gives that call meaning and response. Within the school there will be those who will enter fully and also those who on the other hand will remain spectators. That the Chaplain must be willing to accept.

The second consideration is that schools are intended to be educational: that is to lead young people to think about ideas which can be diverse, difficult and sometimes complicated when one tries to relate them to each other. Further, school seeks to widen and deepen the pupil's experience and perceptions of life. Therefore, while worship is a balance between learning and inspiration within the school, the stress, because of the nature of the community and its function, should weigh more heavily on the learning than the inspiration. This does not mean that one excludes the other.

The acceptance of these considerations helps us to formulate what we can effectively hope to achieve in the school situation. It would suggest that there is always a place for 'stories'—they are liked by all ages of life. This does not mean that the Children's Address of morning worship is the best approach to Primary School Assembly, for the reason that the school cannot and should not be expected to do the work of the Church—that is, the reinforcement of Christian inspiration and attitude previously described. The school requires an approach with greater learning emphasis.

THE LEARNING APPROACH

This directs us to consider seriously the learning approach. The least effective way of teaching, which makes learning possible, is to tell pupils (or, for that matter, anyone) what is good for them to know. We most quickly forget what we hear, compared to what we receive through sight or touch. If what we hear is to be remembered, it must be meaningful. To be meaningful it has to be pegged to our mental framework, our experience, our perspective of the world. If it fails to do this, it is an *inert idea* floating over our life like a cloud. No matter how good or worthy it may be, it passes us by.

Perhaps one of the difficulties facing the Church today is that its framework, perspective, language, is so different from the people outside the Church, that its proclamation has become, for the majority, the transmission of *inert ideas* and seen, therefore, as irrelevant.

To counter this process, school takes serious account of the development stages through which pupils pass from childhood to adulthood. School endeavours to relate its directed learning in ways and words appropriate to pupils at a particular stage. It resists the temptation to try to teach too much, too soon. It doesn't ask pupils to grapple with concepts which are far ahead of their developmental stage. This principle is self evident in the physical domain of life, where we do not expect young children to carry a burden beyond their ability. So often in the domain of the

110

mind, we are happy to overload them with profound doctrine.

School also, rather than proclaiming conceptual truths, prefers to create learning situations for pupils. Through these, as participators, pupils come to realise for themselves the issues of concern and so begin to work towards their own solutions and understanding. The most effective learning comes from what we actually do and experience for ourselves.

If our provision of school worship is to be effective, it too must take account of the developmental stages of pupils and create learning situations for pupil participation. It is these that should shape for us the form and content of Assembly.

MULTI-RELIGIOUS SCHOOLS

Before proceeding to consider such Assemblies, there is another aspect of the general school scene to be considered. Many schools, particularly in the Central belt of Scotland as well as elsewhere, have pupils who are the children of devout Muslim, Hindu or Sikh families, and who desire that their children grow in their particular faith. Such children are Scottish, whose parents themselves were born in Scotland. They are not immigrants.

This fact makes Scotland and Scottish schools multi-faith communities. The fact that it does not apply to all Scottish schools does not exempt any school from understanding this aspect of Scottish life, and how religions other than Christianity affect the lives of fellow Scots.

Chaplains have to recognise this situation and balance the task of being the Christian representative to the school community with that of being Chaplain to the whole school community. Schools are unlikely to welcome Assemblies that fragment the school community into various religious and non-religious segments because of the presence of the Chaplain. This consideration affects what the Chaplain can most effectively offer.

FORMS OF ASSEMBLY

This brings us back to consider the form and content of assembly.

Traditional Form

This has been to conduct a Christian service of worship, similar to a church service, incorporating hymns, prayers, scripture reading, with an appropriate address (the Children's Address!)
We make some observations:

1 This overall structure may be alien to the experience of many of the pupils and staff, especially those who are non-religious or believers in a faith other than Christianity.

2 If the one Assembly embraces the *whole* school, Primary 1-7 (*ie* P1-P7) or Secondary (S1-S6), or even the largest part of the school (P3-P7 or S1-S4), it fails to take account of pupil learning stages and so makes effective communication difficult.

3 If pupils have no other experience, they may find it very difficult to relate to ritual, symbolism, the language of worship, which makes the exercise less than helpful.

Such comments are not to deny that in some schools with particular Chaplains there may be a charisma that can make such an Assembly memorable. That acknowledged, it still remains that as a progressive directed learning approach to worship initiation, it is not the most effective.

Alternative Form

Is there an alternative? Let us begin by rejecting worship as the basic concept for Assembly, on account of the difficulties it presents in the diverse school community, with its demands upon individual faith and commitment to give it reality. Let us start with a more general concept which can lead to and express worship: namely, the concept of *Celebration*.

Celebration is common to religious and non-religious alike. The motivation of the individual participating, if founded on religious belief, will transform the Celebration to religious worship. To the non-religious it will be the expression of human response. Celebration, thus enables us to bridge, in a way all can share, the diverse nature of the school community, respecting individual interpretation and response in a common Assembly.

Celebration opens to us the great common experiences of life at both an individual and community level. Religious communities celebrate key experiences, for example Christians—Christmas and Easter; Muslim—Eid; Hindu—Divali. Cultures celebrate national events—like Armistice Day; also the natural order—like spring or autumn festivals, public holidays. And of course they mark personal family experiences—like celebrations of birth, marriage and death. Festivals may be classed as follows:

1	Religious	Easter, Eid, Divali
2	Life themes	Light, Peace
3	Cultural themes	Burns' Night, St Andrew's Day, other National Events
4	Personal/Family	Birthdays, Weddings

They open a wide world of content and offer flexibility of format as a basis for Assembly. All of which opens possibilities for enlightening, exciting Assemblies.

Chaplain's Caveat

If the celebration of a particular Assembly marks an event of a religion other than Christianity, the Christian Chaplain, as representative of the Christian community, may not wish to actively participate. Others will take the lead role in such an Assembly, but the Chaplain, as a member of the school community, will attend and adopt a spectator role. When a Christian theme is the focus, the Chaplain may take the lead role, while others attend in the role of spectator as members of the school community.

Whatever the role, the attendance is important. It shows oneness with the school community. It affords insight and understanding of the diversity within the community.

THE PRACTICE OF ASSEMBLY

Can such ideas be made to work? Given good will and co-operation between the Head Teacher and the Chaplain, given careful planning and preparation and support with pupils and staff—undoubtedly, yes.

Let us think further of how it may be done by considering the following essential aspects.

Preliminary Preparation

An Assembly Celebration begins with discussion between the Chaplain and Head Teacher. This should achieve mutual understanding of what is planned (in general principle at this stage), the method of implementation and the respective roles to be undertaken by both Chaplain and Head Teacher.

The Chaplain will tend to the supportive role, offering guidance, suggestions and resources, to both the planning committee and pupil participants. The Head Teacher will be responsible for the implementation, arranging meetings of the staff who will participate in planning the Assembly, and making it possible for class time to be given for pupil preparation for participation.

Co-operation and Participation

An Assembly Celebration in which pupils are actively to participate is best achieved by the appointment of a small group of teachers, meeting with the Chaplain, possible the local authority Adviser in Religious Education and the Head Teacher, or whoever he or she delegates to have responsibility for the group.

A different group of staff may plan following Assemblies, though some continuity is desirable.

1 The group will agree the range of the Assembly: *ie* P1-P3, P4-P5 *etc;* or S1-S2, or S3-S4 *etc;*
2 It will decide the theme for Celebration: *eg* Peace, Holidays *etc;*
3 And they will agree the format of the Assembly. See the following examples:

SECONDARY SCHOOL

Programme—Number of items, say 12

Music—3 items	Accompanied by school orchestra/group/instrumental section/audience participation. Music can be from any source that helps theme, not just hymns or religious music.
Drama—2 items	Role-play situation or playlet: Pupils' own work, script-writing, performance, staging *etc* to be encouraged, although other work may also be used.
Visual—3 items	Movement/Dance/Poster/Placards: *eg* MY IDEA OF PEACE IS 'NO WAR'! Pupils to provide.
Audio/Slide —*Presentation*	Use of photography/film/video to express theme.

| *Contributions*—2 | Chaplain 1 Head Teacher 1 |
| *Linking Script*— | Link items of programme. Welcome audience. Introduce theme. Use 1 or perhaps 2 pupi presenters. |

PRIMARY SCHOOL

The Primary school will follow a similar pattern, the staff group deciding the theme and format. In the case of Primary, if the Assembly caters for lower, middle and upper school, a lead class may be chosen for a particular Assembly—then a different lead class for subsequent Assemblies.

The lead class with be given the theme and asked to present it to the Assembly in a variety of ways. Other classes of the Assembly grouping will support by preparing, for example, a frieze for the Assembly hall on the theme, or by participative responses when called, or by sharing music *etc*. (See full Exemplar B which follows on page 119.)

GENERAL POINTS

1 Pupils should help to prepare the hall visually for Assembly.

2 Each pupil and member of staff attending Secondary Assembly, should have a copy of the programme, including words to be sung. In some cases this may also apply to Primary.

3 Preparation of items for Assembly has to be in class time by arrangement of Head Teacher and particular class teacher. A year Assembly in Secondary (for example *all* S1) makes this easier and manageable, although depending on the size of the school it may be better to take S1-S2. Class teachers from the chosen group (say S1) should all participate with respective S1 classes, whether they are members of the planning group or not.

Obviously what is expected of a particular class has to be clearly stated.

4 The preparation is the opportunity for pupils to think about, discuss and face the challenge of a theme. The presentation of these before their peers fosters skills of communication and self-confidence, so increasing the educational value of the exercise.

5 The Chaplain could helpfully be involved and share in such preparation.

PRESENTATION

1 The actual Assembly will be timed to last one period in Secondary school, which will include the movement of classes to and from the hall.

2 Primary will determine an appropriate length.

3 Individual programme items require to be timed.

4 The hall will be arranged so that classes can move easily and freely to participate, while others form the congregation.

5 Each attender will have a copy of the programme. (Secondary Assembly only.)

6 Hall environment—decoration through artwork, artefacts *etc* helps to create atmosphere.

What is important is that the presentation is a Celebration in which all present can actively share, and to which they can individually respond.

It is not a theatrical performance to be constantly rehearsed, nevertheless it must be prepared, spontaneous, worthy of the theme. It is this balance that determines its impact and challenge, and may make it the threshold of worship.

Examples

The following are examples of the Assembly Celebration in both Primary and Secondary schools:

Example A: Primary 6-7

Theme	Passover.
Presentation	By lead class, or each class in P6-P7 making its contribution.

STORYLINE	ACTIVITY
Introduction	Jewish type music.
Story of Passover —that is *then* (see later for *now*)	Dramatise story–acting/role play emphasise (a) slavery, (b) longing for freedom, (c) Promise of deliverance (false hopes) (d) haste of departure. (*Play music.*)
Passover Today	Role-play–search for yeast.
How family celebrate feast	Setting the table, Children carry elements, place on table. Serve unleavened bread and herbs to congregation. Explain the order of eating, drinking and significance. (*Play music.*)
Communion Service (now)	
Development in Christian Church	How Passover relates to Communion. Explain elements and their significance. (*Music.*)

EXAMPLE B: SECONDARY 1

Theme	Peace.
Narrator(s)–Pupil(s)	
Visual presentation	Slide/music, video—depict aspects of peace.
Music	Peace theme.
S1A Drama	Peace in the home.
S1B Ideas of peace	'I THINK PEACE IS'-placard with each pupil's idea. (*Parade so audience can see–complete half circle*).
S1C Symbols of peace	Lotus flower, white dove, pipe, white flag *etc.* (*Pupils display these, and they may possibly be left as a collage at the front of the hall.*)
Music	Ensemble.
S1D Drama	Peace (*industrial/wartime scenario*)
Group S1 Dance	Expression through movement.
Chaplain Christian Peace	Reflect Christian ideas.
S1E Poems	Pupil: peace poetry.
Head Teacher	
Music	Audience participate.

(For further Examples, see RECOMMENDED RESOURCES, p 120.)

CHAPLAIN'S ROLE

In the traditional pattern of Assembly, referred to earlier as a mini church service, the Chaplain's role was to select the theme, choose appropriate hymns, prayers readings and address, and to present the service.

In the alternative model outlined above, the Chaplain's role is to be the facilitator of a celebration that leads to the threshold of worship. The emphasis is on preparation–with staff and pupils–but this allows opportunities to share thoughts, to discuss and establish relationships and rapport. Not only is this good education, but it is also the foundation of good pastoral ministry. Within the Assembly the Chaplain can also make his own individual contribution.

The present role falls more heavily on the pupil than the Chaplain, although his support and encouragement are invaluable.

The alternative uses Assembly themes from the types indicated, but as they arise from the school community. Their use expresses pupil's involvement and concerns and so helps their motivation and perspective of relevance.

Given the nature of schools and the changes in society's attitude to institutional religion, the role suggested above is more likely to be helpful and effective for the decade of the 90s compared with its traditional forebear.

Certainly, while its demands are different, so also is the satisfaction it can bring.

RECOMMENDED RESOURCES

Carrie, John: *It's Their Assembly* (Church of Scotland Video).
Strathclyde Region: *Practical Advice for Multi-cultural Assemblies 1 Primary, 2 Secondary.*